Endorse...

It breaks your heart! Any time you talk about "shattered dreams" you know there is someone, maybe many, who will forever be putting back together the pieces of a broken relationship. Yvonne and Joanne know all about that, but in spite of their similar experiences they refuse to live their lives in self-pity and defeat. They have chosen to get well, and in turn, use their journey to help others find wholeness. Like the ladies say, to "focus on the happy ending."

—**H.B. London, Jr.**
Vice President, Church & Clergy
Focus on the Family

It's always a tragedy when marriage ends in divorce, but when it happens at the parsonage, an entire church body is sent reeling. Joanne and Yvonne portray with honesty and transparency how they strove to protect their congregations while experiencing personal devastation at the hands of their pastor-husbands. Heart-wrenching, yet purposeful, this book reveals a God who brings recovery and healing whenever we trust in Him.

—**Sharon M. Knudson**
Co-Author
Starting from Scratch When You're Single Again

Four young people entered ministry with high hopes and dreams. Two families were formed with an eye on God's will. Step by step, the hopes and dreams died, and the families were left in ruin. In a quiet style, Joanne and Yvonne target what destroys great ministries, great churches, and great families. Nothing is held back. This book will be a comfort to those who are victims of secret sins, but I believe this should be required reading for those who dare to enter ministry.

—**John Walsh**
Author of *The Art of Storytelling*
President of Christian Storytelling Network

Adultery is devastating. When it occurs in a ministry family living in the proverbial "glass house," the pain and loss are magnified immeasurably. *Surviving Shattered Dreams* recounts the stories of two wives married to pastors who destroyed themselves, their homes, and their ministries with adulterous affairs. Yet these brave women survived—and recovered with grace to continue serving the Lord! The book tells how. Everyone will benefit from the practical insights and biblical wisdom woven into it. Compelling reading!

—**Galen Call**
Senior Pastor
Venture Christian Church, Los Gatos, CA

Surviving Shattered Dreams is a book about desperation, humiliation, and deep soul searching. It's about ministry leaders who are posers . . . the pain they inflict, and the festering emotional wounds they leave. But it's also about hope, courage, God's faithfulness, and life after tragedy. The twin stories weave a tapestry of grief and betrayal that is transformed into a rich display of God's sustaining grace. An ongoing dialogue between the authors opens up life lessons and preventive steps, both for individuals and churches who wrestle with issues of accountability. You will not read this with dry eyes. My emotions ranged from sympathy to anger, from sorrow to grief, from despair to resolve. You will see the horrific scars from the mutilation and amputation done to Christ's body. Ministry wives will find strength to stand for truth; children of dysfunctional ministry homes, who are sick of the pulpit-parsonage disparity, will find they are not alone; and for men who live in or near the swampland of deceit, the alarm sounds with penetrating decibels. With highest respect for the women who with incredible transparency reveal their immeasurable hurt and process of healing, I recommend this book as a must read. "I have refined you, but not as silver is refined. Rather, I have refined you in the furnace of suffering" (Isa. 48:10 NLT).

—**Rev. Stephen LeBar**, Ph.D.
Executive Director, Conservative Baptist Association

I know Joanne and Yvonne, and I know their story. *Surviving Shattered Dreams* is the frightening and ugly journey of two women, faithful to God, but who experienced the severe pain of clergy husbands who kept neither their marriage vows nor their promises to God.

This is much more than a story of personal survival. It is the story of hurt, abandonment, and even worse, how each of them saw their trusting children suffer horribly as well.

Does God see when men leave behind their clerical facade and enter their own dark world when they return to their homes? How can God allow such brutal and even unspeakable things to happen to the wives and children of those who lead the church?

As Joanne and Yvonne show us in *Surviving Shattered Dreams,* God is neither blind nor absent. His presence, love, and undergirding strength were there and brought these two women and their children through their darkest of nights and into effective ministries of helping others.

I know that, sadly, Joanne and Yvonne are not alone. Others reading these pages will be quietly saying, "Thank God, somebody knows what I'm facing." Then there may come the realization that "if God can help these women in their situation, maybe God can help me in mine." Perhaps through their own tears and feelings of desperation, readers will find a kinship with these women and realize that there is hope and that there is a way through to the love and light and peace of God that really does pass all human understanding.

This is more than a book for personal reading, although it will reach into the soul of each reader. It is also a book to share with others and to discuss in a group. I hope that it will help people in the churches to become alert to any who have been suffering secretly and who inwardly are crying out to God.

The authors of *Surviving Shattered Dreams* are honest, transparent, personal, and deep. When the last page is turned, I believe that the reader will have been touched not only by Joanne's and Yvonne's stories but also by God.

—**Roger Palms**
Former editor, *Decision* Magazine

Read this book. It's like talking with your closest girlfriend.

—**Mary Fran Heitzman**
Co-Author
Starting from Scratch When You're Single Again

Surviving
Shattered
Dreams

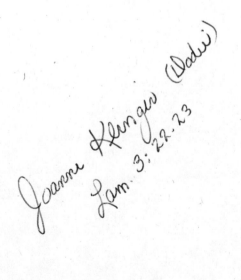

Yvonne Partyka & Joanne Klinger

Surviving
Shattered
Dreams

A STORY OF HOPE AFTER DESPAIR

WinePress **WP** Publishing™

WinePress Publishing (PO Box 428, Enumclaw, WA 98022) functions only as book publisher. As such, the ultimate design, content, editorial accuracy, and views expressed or implied in this work are those of the author.

ISBN 13: 978-1-57921-984-0
ISBN 10: 1-57921-984-5
Library of Congress Catalog Card Number: 2008933081

Contents

Acknowledgments

Blessings to our daughters:
Joanne's: Sarah, Emily, and Alexi
Kari (with the Lord)
Yvonne's: Beth and Anne
You make our lives full!

Bill, you are a blessing and a wonderful support.
I love you with all my heart. You helped heal a broken one.
Thank you for believing in us as we wrote this book. *Love, Yvonne*

Roger and Andrea, your friendship is worthy of honor.
Your encouragement kept us going on this project.

Thank you to our many friends
who believed in us.

Thank you to all the people at WinePress:
Abigail, Adam, Athena, Carla, George, Mike, Roger, and Simon

Thank you to all the men and women in ministry
who remain so faithful to the task.
You are exceptional!
Thank you, again and again.

Thank you LORD!
You are the reason we exist.
Your faithfulness is what this book is about.

Our Marriage

It was a beautiful, fragile vase,
And I held its delicate form in my hands,
Gently and tenderly.
The colors glowed in a pattern of happiness
And shimmered softly in the evening hours.
It was a treasure I cared for with great pleasure
And placed it where all could enjoy its beauty.
One day I noticed a crack—just a slight one—
And I turned it so the small marring of its beauty
Would not be visible to others.
As the years went by, many new homes
Held the vase, and each time I lifted it
Out of its wrappings, I saw
More and more cracks
Breaking through the colors,
Changing their pattern of happiness
To scars of sorrow.
Now all could see
That the vase was broken
and useless.
One day I picked it up,
And it fell apart in my hands.
I held the broken fragments
With bleeding fingers
And wept.

Joanne Klinger

CHAPTER 1

Is this Really Happening?

My world collapses

Joanne:

I heard his voice but it seemed surreal. I responded as I'd always done when Greg attacked me verbally. My mind shut down, and I couldn't speak or think. I just had to wait until he was through. But this time, I had the presence of mind to ask our twenty-one-year-old daughter, Emily, to come into the room and listen to her father. By this time, Greg was in such an irrational state that he didn't even notice her.

"I may as well give up trying to have any kind of ministry"; he fired his anger and accusations at me in rapid succession. "Every time I get something going, you leave, and it all goes out the window. We are supposed to be a team, but you constantly change your mind and turn against me."

As always, he blamed me for everything bad that had happened to us—the loss of our ministry, the loss of our home, and his inability to pastor a church.

"I'm going for a walk," he said, and abruptly left.

I turned to Emily. "If he is right, then I'm nothing but a worm, not even worthy of living. I think I'm crazy. Maybe I should just die."

She grabbed my shoulders. "Mom, it's not you, it's him. You are not crazy."

She persisted until I realized that once again I had almost allowed his attack to destroy me.

I finally decided I could not stay in this marriage. For twenty-seven years I had endured Greg's verbal attacks and temper outbursts his lying, justifying an affair, and hiding pornography. I had left three times in the past ten years, but returned thinking that if I could just be a better wife I could hold this marriage together. Greg could then stay in the ministry he always insisted God had called him to. Each time I went back, it confirmed to Greg that he did not have any problems. In his mind, I was the problem. I knew leaving this time meant I would never return.

Greg's irrational outbursts had started shortly after we were married. I never knew what would cause them. If I forgot to double bag the groceries and one broke when he lifted it out of the car, he would scream at me. If we set a time to meet somewhere and I was a minute late, he would fly into a tirade. Every outburst from him caused me to shrivel up inside. However, I never considered separation or divorce, having been taught that Christians don't end their marriages for any reason.

Later, I discovered pornographic materials hidden in his desk. Then he grudgingly admitted he was having an affair with a church member, but only after lying to me about it on several occasions. Even after he began controlling our four children through anger, I still did not consider divorce. By that time I felt obligated to maintain the appearance of a "wonderful Christian family in ministry" for the sake of the church. I felt trapped and hopeless. Counseling was not even a possibility. Why would the successful pastor of a large and growing church need counseling? After all, he was the counselor. He always had answers for others.

I tried not to think about how much the stress in our home might be affecting the girls. I ignored the fear I often saw in their faces. Kari withdrew into books, and Alexi spent most of her time at home, shut in her bedroom. I knew she was hiding from the tension that came in the front door with Greg. I didn't know then, but I found out later that Greg had also been abusing the girls.

The paradox between life at church and life at home became normal living. It's easier to pretend problems don't exist if there is no way to solve them. *Maybe tomorrow will be better*, I continually thought.

My emotions were frozen. When women confided in me and sought advice and comfort for problems, I felt no compassion. When my mother—whom I loved dearly—died of breast cancer, I couldn't cry. I felt guilty that I had no tears, but I could not feel the loss. I was only worried that my husband might cause trouble for the family. He had had conflicts in the past with my father and my two brothers-in-law.

My life was consumed with avoiding mistakes so I could sidestep the emotional scenes and outbursts of temper. Someone once said, "A double life always merges into a single reality at some point." I was deathly afraid this would happen to me.

I left that night for the final time before Greg returned from his walk. But the wounds were raw and bleeding, and I knew I needed professional help if there was any chance of healing. I didn't even know if I could live independently. The thought of finding a job, renting an apartment, and getting a car overwhelmed me.

At fifty years old, I was still recovering from a hip joint replacement due to arthritis and was in constant pain. I never visualized my life in this way. My goals and dreams were now shattered bits and pieces lying all around me.

My prayer life changed immediately. In Psalm 12:1, the first two words that David spoke were, "Help, Lord. . . ." In my Bible, I wrote above those words, "a great prayer." I prayed, "Help, Lord, I need the physical strength to go job hunting."

"Help, Lord, I need to find a place to live."

"Help, Lord, I need to find a good counselor."

"Help, Lord, I need money to live on right now."

"Help, Lord, I need to be strong for my girls."

He answered every prayer.

I soon found a good Christian counselor, and the first time I met with him, I huddled in a chair and sobbed for an hour. In answer to prayer, friends gave me money to put a deposit down on an apartment.

I found a job teaching fifth grade in a Christian school connected to the church we once pastored, so I worked with friends and people I knew. They proved to be a great support group. But life still wasn't easy. I continued to feel weak and helpless.

Two of my daughters moved with me into the apartment. Emily was out of college and working, so we split the cost of the apartment, utilities, and groceries. My youngest daughter, Alexi, had just graduated from high school and was preparing to go to college in the fall. She was angry and hurt by all that had happened in our family, but agreed to live with me in the apartment. Sarah, the eldest, was living and working in another city. Kari was married and lived about three hundred miles away.

Creating a home environment can be very comforting. I was thankful for the relief from constant fears and worries that kept circling my mind like hunting dogs that had treed a raccoon. They threatened to drag me down into depression and prevent me from functioning at any moment.

The prophet Jeremiah wrote in Lamentations: ". . . my soul is downcast within me, yet this I call to mind and therefore I have hope: Because of the Lord's great love we are not consumed, because his compassions never fail. They are new every morning; great is your faithfulness" (Lam. 3:20–23).

Those words were my "tree" of safety and comfort. I hung onto them whenever fears and depression tried to drag me down.

At times I felt so full of grief and pain that I did not see how I could go on. I wanted to curl up on my bed, throw a blanket over my head, and disappear from the world. I felt the death of my marriage as keenly as if someone I loved had died. I wrestled with guilt over walking away, while realizing that our marriage had died long before I left.

Friends would say, "Now you can move on." That sounds healthy, but I would ask myself, *What does that mean?* I had moved on in a physical sense: I had a job, I had a place to live, I was breathing and alive, but I couldn't stop feeling fractured, abandoned, and robbed of the goals and dreams I once had.

Yvonne:

"Yvonne, I know this isn't good timing, but I have something to tell you," my husband, Ted, said. "I'm leaving you and the girls. I'll give notice to the church as soon as I can."

Even after all these years, I still vividly remember that day.

"Don't try to talk me out of anything. I've been thinking about this for a while, and I've made up my mind. You'll have to tell the girls," Ted added.

We were sitting in Ted's study, a cozy room off the living room. The sun shone brightly, and snow covered the hillside. I loved to come here and talk with him. It was a special room, filled with books and memories. It was a symbol of our shared lives and ministries. I had assumed our conversation would be about this evening's Christmas program. I was directing the play and had some last-minute questions. I stared out the window at the frozen creek and bare trees. Suddenly our cozy room grew cold, as if exposed to a wintry blast of air. The cold pierced my heart. I heard the remoteness in Ted's voice, as if he were talking about someone else's life.

How could this be happening to me? Rushing to his chair, I crouched on the floor in front of him. Normally a calm, in-control person, I felt completely lost. "You can't do this! You can't do this!" I sobbed.

Ted pushed me away and said, "Yes I can. You can't stop me."

My thoughts were a jumble of questions. *Can I talk him out of this?* We had worked through problems before. *What can I do to stop him? Maybe I can change. What does he want from me?* I felt threatened, alone, unwanted. *What have I done to deserve this? I won't survive!*

I looked out the window, and the barren hillside stared back at me. How could the sun still be shining? I felt like I was in the middle of a freak tornado, being tossed in every direction. I visualized the girls and myself as trees being torn up from the roots and flying through the air. My whole world was being ripped apart.

Then, just as quickly, I felt a sense of calmness that could come only from God; the God who loved me wrapped his loving arms around me. I returned to my chair to prepare for the long conversation that was to come. I knew in my heart that I could never control Ted's life. Nor was I in control of my own life. Someone greater than I would need to take over.

On this tumultuous afternoon, Ted confessed to adulterous affairs over the past six months. He also shared thoughts he'd been wrestling with. As I listened, some of the confusion lifted that I had been feeling over our marriage.

I knew he had not been well physically and was burning out. He was disgruntled with his workload and the people around him. I sensed his walk with God lacked the closeness he once had.

The affairs were not a complete surprise. Ted had been emotionally distant from me for some time. Suspicious that he was cheating, I had accused him of having an affair on several occasions. That afternoon he gave me bits and pieces, but no straight answers. He said the marriage was over. He needed to rest. He would resign from the church and go to his brother's home for a few months, until he could make future plans. Ironically, he also tried to comfort me.

"Yvonne, this isn't personal. You've been a good wife and mother."

What does he mean? Of course this is personal!

"It's just that I'm not in love with you anymore. Being with other women makes me want more."

I bristled. "I'm confused. What's going on? You said it was over." *If it is really over, why is he leaving me now?* "Please, Ted. Love is a choice. Feelings come and go. Don't we have anything?" *Who is he in love with? There has got to be more going on here than he's telling me.*

"Yvonne, I want a new life. I'm tired of pretending to be someone I'm not."

He sounds exhausted. Maybe all he needs is a good rest.

"I'm leaving the ministry. I'll find a career where they'll pay me what I'm worth."

What? I thought we were content here.

"I've given up my life for this, and it's over."

He seemed to have no sense of remorse for what this would mean to the church family. *Wasn't he called to be their shepherd?* I felt the weight of this responsibility on my shoulders. *It doesn't seem to be bothering him at all.* "What about the girls?" I pleaded. "Maybe I can handle this pain, but what about them? I need you. The girls need you. More than ever. At thirteen and fourteen, they need their father!"

"I gave them the best years of my life. They will be all right," he said tersely. The tone of his voice was one I'd seldom heard. It sounded bitter, sarcastic, and selfish. It made no sense to me and sent chills down my spine.

How can you say that? I screamed in my head. We had often talked about the teen years and how important the father/daughter relationship is to healthy development. We had worked with teenagers for the past fifteen years. Somehow his words rang hollow, like a cracked bell. I knew he was going against everything he believed. I would soon find out reasons behind this twisted thinking, but at this point, I was completely in the dark.

Oh, God, this can't be happening! But it was. And I was still in charge of the evening's program. My voice trembled. "You're the one who has to tell the girls. You can't pass that responsibility off! You need to face them." Realizing the time, I continued. "I suggest you talk to them tomorrow— they won't be able to handle the evening if you tell them now."

My thoughts turned to the program that evening. The play I was directing told of the shepherds who witnessed the birth of Jesus, his life, death, and resurrection. Responsibility kicked in, as it usually did. I don't remember how I managed to get through the evening. I do remember the Christmas program went beautifully.

I marveled that in spite of my inner turmoil, life could go on so normally all around me. I was still inspired that our Lord, born as a baby, would someday pay for the sins of the world. I marveled at the resurrection; it still stirred my heart. As the shepherds played their roles, some believed and others questioned. They also spoke to my heart, and I knew, again, that the God who could become incarnate could reach into my broken heart.

Joanne and Yvonne:

We knew our marriages were ended—and life as we knew it. Neither of us was certain we could go on. Our dreams of a happy, loving home, building memories with our children, growing old together, and teamwork in ministry were all shattered. The goals we had talked about with our husbands would never happen.

We wondered how many other families have been fractured or ripped apart by these same issues. We believe Satan wants to destroy the credibility of leadership in the church. He would like nothing better than to destroy from within.

There are people in full-time ministry who live double lives that are never exposed. Could it be possible that our stories could help families in crisis deal with issues before those issues destroy their homes and the testimony of the church? Are there women who are in pain because they feel they can't talk to anyone? Are there people who have given up on the church or are deeply hurt by what they have witnessed within the church?

Yvonne and I met when she was training me to fill the position she had held for six years at a church. God had worked it out so that I would have employment near my daughter, who had just been diagnosed with an inoperable brain tumor. The more we talked, the more a bond of friendship quickly built in our hearts, and we have been friends ever since. In the weeks and months that followed, we discussed questions that troubled us as we struggled to survive not only the betrayal in our marriages but also the ramifications of other secrets that would soon come to light. Because of our shared experiences, we had empathy and understanding for each other.

Questions continually raced through our minds. *Is this really happening? Is there anything I can do to "fix" this? If I had been a better marriage partner, would things be different? How will I make a living? How will this affect the girls? What will people say?*

Probably the question that nagged us the most was: How did I end up like this when the beginning of my marriage seemed so bright and happy and full of promise?

CHAPTER 2

"Do You Take this Man?"

The ministry dream

Joanne:

This was it—my wedding day! I stood waiting with my father at the top of the gently sloping aisle and looking toward the front of the church auditorium. My heart pounded with excitement and happiness. I slipped my hand through my father's arm as he looked down at my face and whispered, "You look beautiful, honey; it's time to go!"

We started slowly down the aisle, and I heard the rustle of my satiny, white wedding dress as I moved toward the man standing at the front of the church, the man who was going to help make my goals and dreams come true.

Greg and I first met in college, through a mutual friend. It was my senior year and his junior year. He had served in the army before coming to school. It was the end of the '50s, and going to college for many had two purposes—to obtain a college degree and to find a mate. A girl who entered the last semester of her senior year without getting engaged saw her chances of marriage greatly diminish, or so we thought. I had dated a few times but had had no serious relationships. It looked as though I was going to graduate without a ring on my finger. And where in the world would I meet a future husband if I couldn't find one at a Christian college?

Then my friend Jan introduced me to Greg. Jan was beautiful, smart, and was liked by everyone. She was voted homecoming queen our senior year, and she was engaged to a football player. She also was very serious about her relationship with God. We often spent late nights sprawled out on twin beds discussing our lives, our beliefs, our dreams, and our struggles.

"You and Greg would be great together," she teased me one night. "If I let him know you are interested, would you go out with him sometime?"

"Sure," I said. "I don't have any ring on my finger—yet." We both laughed as Jan quickly put her left hand behind her back and tried to look sympathetic.

Several days later, Greg asked me to go to a Sunday night church service with him. We drove out to a little church in the country, where a friend of his was the pastor. Small talk has never come easily to me, and I was nervous about what to say. I didn't need to worry, because Greg kept the conversation going. He told me about his time in the army, which made it possible to attend college on the GI Bill. He also said he wanted to be a pastor, and I thought to myself, *Could he be the man I will marry?* After all, my father was a pastor, and I was right at home in church ministry.

I spent most of my childhood buried in books. Living in the world of romance and idealism came naturally to me. I imagined what my life would be like if I married this man. My degree was in elementary education, so I could teach school while Greg went to seminary, and then together we could pastor a church somewhere and raise a family. We would both be serving God in ministry. I even pictured the rose-covered, white-picket parsonage fence!

As our relationship continued, I was impressed when Greg suggested we pray on our dates and take on the challenge of memorizing a book of the Bible together. We chose 1 John because it was short and the pattern of the book was easy to follow. Whenever we were riding in Greg's car, we listened to each other recite what we had learned. Our praying was centered on asking God to show us his will for the future. Greg's desire for us to study the Bible and combine it with prayer seemed to confirm that he was the right fit for my dreams and goals.

After graduating, I found a job in the fall teaching in a public grade school. I went home for the summer, three hundred miles away, and Greg stayed in the area, working full time. We wrote letters, made many phone calls, and he drove to my home on several weekends. I was in love with the love letters that came every other day and in love with the knowledge that I was with someone who told me constantly that he loved me.

The letters always talked about how beautiful I was and seemed to focus on physical attraction; I felt secure and wanted. I knew I was not as physically attractive as he seemed to see me, but I loved being told these things. Better yet, I was no longer a single—I was a couple! I felt I now belonged with my peer group.

Before Greg and I started dating, I did not like the prospect of being single. *What kind of life am I going to have, living all alone and teaching children year after year? I might end up being the proverbial old-maid schoolteacher!* Most of the adults I knew back home were married people. My older sister had just married her college boyfriend. All around me, senior girls were flashing engagement rings. As underclassmen, we often joked about "senior panic" as we watched couples getting engaged. Now I didn't have to worry about that.

We were married the following summer, after Greg's graduation. We moved to the Midwest so he could attend seminary. Everything was turning out exactly as I had dreamed. I was no longer facing life alone, and I was the wife of a pastor-in-training. We would soon be serving God in full-time ministry. I was sure a church was just waiting for us!

I took another teaching job, and we rented a one-bedroom apartment. For several weeks I "played house" and had fun using all our new wedding gifts to make the apartment a cozy home.

Then reality began to rip out the pages of my storybook romance.

Yvonne:

I noticed him the first week of school. I had just entered my freshman year at a well-known Bible school. Alphabetical seating often brought us close in the classroom. Soon my roommate and I began sitting with Ted and his roommate and a few other friends for meals. Ted and I knew we liked each other.

I wanted him to ask me out. Yet he seemed distant. During the first semester we began to take walks together. He was respectful of me. We would stop at the lounge of my dorm and pray together before we said "good night." We read *Pilgrim's Progress* together during that first year. We were doing things together as a couple, but I was never sure where our relationship was going.

Since I had never dated in high school, I wasn't certain what to expect. My parents had raised me with strong moral values. The boys I would have liked to date didn't seem to know I existed. The boys who did ask were after more than friendship. I said "no."

I was what Ted later called "young, naïve, and innocent." I expected that we would hold hands and kiss, yet there was none of that at the beginning. The lack of physical touch confused me. I distinctly remember the first walk when we held hands. It was wonderful. I knew we were more than just friends. I can also remember our first kiss, gentle and soft, not forceful. I felt assured this was more than just a casual friendship.

Ted had always had girl problems in high school. He would tell me how frustrated his mother would get with him when one girl was going out the back door as another came in the front. I thought this was comical, and we laughed together. He told me that he struggled with keeping his dating relationships pure. There were many girls and many problems. What he didn't tell me was whether or not he had been sexually active. He kept secret any details that might change our relationship.

Ted told me after we were engaged that he had picked me to date because of my innocence. He also admitted that he was not attracted to me physically and had decided that I would be a great date because it would help him keep his hormones and emotions under control. He respected me and wanted to build a relationship right this time.

My heart sank. *Should I be insulted? Should I be glad?* I heard his explanations with mixed emotions. *Maybe I should walk right out of this relationship. I want him to be attracted to me physically. God, is that so wrong?* I remembered the stories my parents told me about when they first met. The attraction was one-sided, but it developed into a beautiful romance. I thought of others I had known where physical attraction had taken time.

I told myself none of this mattered. I knew that building a relationship on values, dreams, and like interests was much more important than physical attraction. I also knew that physical attraction could interfere with getting to know each other well. We did love each other, we both loved the Lord, and we made a great team.

I wanted more physical touch with Ted but had no idea that it would escalate so fast. When we started with longer kisses, it soon led to heavy kissing and petting. I did not know where to draw appropriate boundaries. I did, however, know that sexual intimacy was wrong outside of marriage. I have often asked myself, *If I had known Ted's background would I have dated him in the first place?* I'll never know, but I do suspect he believed honesty about his past would end our relationship.

I entered marriage making the huge assumption that we were both virgins. Marriage brought relief from sexual tension and gave us a sense of fulfillment. We prayed together and worked together. I believed that my husband was the person he portrayed himself to be. But deception on his part coupled with my innocence created a world where he could take advantage of my faith in him.

As an engaged couple, we attended a six-week marriage counseling course provided by our school. Ted and I were married right after graduation and relocated in order to allow him to continue his education. We worked as volunteer youth sponsors in our local church, helping the group grow from a few teens to forty. Beth was born the following year and Anne the next.

When Ted accepted his first full-time ministry position as a youth pastor, we moved across the country. We were in a fairly large church, where he worked under other staff. I helped in the youth department, and together we shared successful and enjoyable ministry. However, Ted often struggled with the list of expectations the youths' parents had for him. He often remarked, "You know what these parents want? They want me to 'fix' their kids. The responsibility really lies with them!" Disillusionment was taking its toll. It was not easy for him to deal with the politics of working with other staff. So he resigned with the intent of finding a position as a pastor.

Soon after, Ted received a call to pastor a country church. He told me that he would "rather be a large frog in a little pond than a little frog in a large pond." We looked forward to this new challenge.

What a wonderful experience this pastorate was. We loved the people. Since we had both grown up in the country, our hearts were content with country living and country folks. We were again building a youth group, and the teens were growing spiritually. Ted was ordained at this church. One of our parishioners said with a drawl, "Never seen so many big guns all in one place before!" I was so proud of Ted and his accomplishments. I was grateful to the Lord for choosing us for ministry. My heart was full.

We had several good years and great memories. Little did I see the storm clouds rising on the horizon that threatened to destroy the work and our future.

Joanne and Yvonne:

Yvonne and I sat in front of my computer, sipping hot tea and talking about our college days.

"Joanne, why did you choose a Christian college?"

"Well," I said slowly, "I wanted a good education from an accredited school so I could teach when I graduated. I also knew that if I wanted to find a Christian to marry, my best chances were probably at a Christian school."

"You know what they say," Yvonne interjected, "if you want to fish, you need to go where the fish are!"

I grinned. "You could put it that way. What I was trying to say is that marriage, a family, and some kind of ministry were always part of the life I visualized for myself. Was that wrong?"

"No," she sighed. "Those were my desires, too. My purpose in choosing a Bible school was part of that plan. I wanted to prepare for ministry, but it certainly was a great place to meet guys who were going in the same direction."

Looking back, what did we miss? What was lacking in our knowledge of relationships and marriage that might have helped us to be more discerning? As we talked and jotted down notes, some concepts became very clear.

Faulty perceptions of marriage, common to most young women, prevented us from entering into a relationship with more wisdom. Idealism, romantic unreality, or "head-in-the-clouds" mind-set, and a mixture of truth and untruth in our belief system were all part of our thinking.

We tended to view ourselves as half-persons, looking for someone to complete us. Marriage counselors Les and Leslie Parrott teach that entering into marriage as a whole person, able to function independently and make decisions about life based on more realistic foundations, gives the marriage a much greater chance of succeeding and being fulfilling for both partners.

We were caught up in the "opposites attract" syndrome so natural to the dating process. Being attracted to someone different can be a good thing, but when it is the result of sensing inadequacy in oneself and hoping the other person will fill that need, it's unhealthy. If we had been looking for compatibility instead, we might have lessened the high degree of adjustment required by our differences.

Yvonne and I were both more reserved in social groups. The men we married seemed to have an appealing social confidence. They could make conversation with anyone and were often the life of the party. As Yvonne and I talked, we realized that it was easier for us to fade into the background and become a part of their scene.

This opposites attract idea had another side. We each had strengths that we brought into our respective relationships. We believed these strengths could help overcome our husbands' weaknesses, and that felt good. I came from a fairly healthy family unit. I had felt love, security, and respect from both of my parents. I had been taught biblical truth from the time I was old enough to understand and had become a believer at the age of eight.

Yvonne had also grown up in a loving and stable Christian home and accepted Christ as her Savior at age eleven. She had inherited the determination that says, "I can do this; I can help you; I am the fixer." Both of our families believed in helping others.

Both Greg and Ted had grown up in extremely dysfunctional families, and some unhealthy patterns still influenced their choices and thinking. There was physical and likely sexual abuse in both families. It was common practice to protect family secrets and to live with family lies. Accountability and responsibility were foreign words in these family systems. Some unhealthy patterns were not so obvious at the time we were dating, and some we chose to ignore. Neither Yvonne nor I viewed these differences as serious hindrances to a healthy relationship. After all, Greg and Ted were Christians, and they were not responsible for their families' unhealthiness.

Could we have been more discerning in getting to know our future husbands? Yes, certainly. Yet, Romans 8:28 says, "And we know that all things work together for good to those who love God, to those who are the called according to His purpose" (NKJV). Could not God work in all circumstances to bring about his good in our lives? Our problems were not insurmountable. Or were they? Both Yvonne and I were starting to see an expanding gap between our dreams of sharing life and ministry with a godly partner and the reality that it wasn't turning out that way at all.

CHAPTER 3

Is This the Person I Married?

The dream fades

Joanne:

Looking back, I can see things I should have noticed in our relationship. Growing up at home, I was what a counselor would call a "robot." My father had a placid temperament. The only times when I saw him get angry, he would become quiet and his mouth would tense into a straight line. He treated all of us with love, respect, and firmness, when necessary. However, he was careful to be a good example of a Christian pastor in the community, and he expected us to help uphold that image. I loved my father and determined at an early age that I would never do anything that would hurt him or shame him. I was the "good" girl.

In contrast, Greg grew up in a non-Christian home filled with violence, fear, and abuse. The stories Greg related to me about his home life were beyond my comprehension. His father was a bitter man who controlled the family with his anger, and he passed this behavior on to his children. When I visited Greg's home for the first time, everyone was polite to me, but even though I was quite naïve about family relationships outside of my own family, I could sense the atmosphere in this home was tense. Greg had become a Christian as a teenager and spent more time in his pastor's home than his own, trying to escape the almost daily battles at his house.

Even though Greg's family had problems, I thought he was different. He managed to get himself through college and was headed toward seminary. He was a believer who only wanted to do what he strongly felt God had called him to do. I admired someone who would step away from his kind of home and make right choices. I didn't realize how much that home had crippled him.

Throughout our dating and the months before the wedding, I never saw Greg get angry or show any temper. I was confident that I was marrying a wonderful man, who was fun to be with and who had goals for life that were also my goals. My parents saw the same person I saw and were happy for us. There was no marriage counseling. We assumed that people just got married and went from there, working out the problems along the way.

However, problems began almost immediately after the wedding and honeymoon. My parents agreed to help us get settled in our first apartment. They helped us clean and even went shopping with us for a bed. Greg was ominously quiet while we all picked out the bed and my parents paid for it. In fact he was rudely quiet when I thought he should be thanking them for their help! He told me later that night, when we were alone, "Your parents should stay out of our business! You should stop acting like their little girl!" I was hurt and bewildered at the anger in his voice. Was this the same Greg I had dated?

I soon began to see Greg's volatile, unpredictable anger flare up when situations or people threatened to upset the way life needed to go in order for him to feel in control. I realized that I needed to avoid making mistakes or saying the wrong thing so that I would not have to take the brunt of those angry outbursts. The fear of trying to play it safe created its own stress.

Our first baby was born during Greg's last year in seminary. We were living on campus in the married students' apartment complex. I loved babies, and I was thrilled about being a mother. But Sarah was a fussy baby, and my confidence was shaken when I couldn't quiet her crying. The walls of our apartments were not well insulated. Sometimes at night I could hear the snores of the professor who lived on one side of us. I was worried that Sarah's crying would disturb our neighbors. I was even more worried about upsetting Greg.

The first week we were home with Sarah, I was taking a hot shower one afternoon, trying to get some relief from the pain of giving birth. All of a sudden the door banged open and Greg yelled, "Get out of there right now and take care of this baby; something's wrong with her."

He kept yelling at me to hurry as I stepped out of the shower and wrapped a towel around myself. Sarah was lying on the changing table in our bedroom, crying at the top of her lungs, her face all red and puffy. I picked her up, held her close, and talked soothingly to her.

Suddenly there was a loud knock on our door, and when Greg opened it the young couple across the hall was standing there. "Is something wrong?" they asked with concern. "Can we help?"

"No, we're fine. The baby was just fussing," Greg replied, then shut the door. I knew they had heard him yelling. What did they think of us? There was nothing wrong with Sarah; Greg had been frustrated with her crying while he was trying to change her diaper. Again I felt responsible to fix everything around Greg so that he would not get upset or feel threatened. But how could I control a crying baby?

Coming home from church one Sunday, Sarah was hungry and began to cry. After entering the apartment, I had started to change my clothes when Greg yelled, "Feed her *now* and forget your clothes." The stress and fear I felt inside as I sat naked, nursing my baby could not have been healthy for her.

One night I could not get Sarah to go to sleep. She was just a little over a year old and always had a hard time settling down at night and at naptime. I finally put her in her crib with a bottle, and she fell asleep. In the middle of the night she woke up crying, and nothing seemed to pacify her. Greg woke up angry, then he took her out of her crib and spanked her hard. He then brought her into our bedroom and literally threw her into the bed beside me. He went into the living room and slept on the couch the rest of the night.

Sarah was shaking and crying in great shuddering sobs. I remember thinking, *My baby and I are at the mercy of a person with uncontrollable rage.* I felt terribly alone and helpless. I had this great urge to pack a suitcase and fly home to the safety of my parents, but I didn't have the courage to admit to them what our life was really like. I cuddled Sarah close in my arms and finally felt her body relax as she drifted into sleep, an occasional sob still escaping from her. When I changed her diaper the next morning, I was horrified to see slight bruising. *What if someone notices?*

Greg seemed to put these episodes entirely out of his mind. If I brought one up the next day, he would say it was over and there was no need to discuss it. Or he would look at me as if I were making it up and say, "I don't know what you're talking about."

When Sarah was eighteen months old, Emily was born, eight weeks ahead of her due date. Though tiny, she was a placid and healthy baby. She ate and slept and hardly ever fussed. I was now a very busy mother, caring for two infants. I was being very careful not to upset Greg. I ached for us to be a happy, healthy, functioning Christian family. Even though my dream was fading, I was determined to do everything in my power to make it at least appear real.

After seminary, Greg accepted an invitation to pastor a small country church in Ohio. Most of the people were farmers and, for them, farm work came before church. But Greg was demanding that at least the elders attend every church function, regardless of farming season. He kept pushing, and they kept right on with their livelihood first. One night, his irrational anger reached a point of no return.

I had been asleep for some time when something disturbed me. As a young mother I heard everything that went bump in the night. I sat up in bed and saw Greg pacing the floor.

"What's the matter?" I could already feel a familiar fear tightening the muscles in my body. By now I had learned that Greg could be totally unpredictable in his responses to situations and people. If he felt the least bit threatened, he would lash out like a caged animal. His best friend could be turned into his enemy. There seemed to be no middle ground in any relationship: either you agreed with Greg, or you were evil and wrong.

"Those elders are either going to work with me or they are going to get off the board. I will personally remove them!"

The next thing I knew, he was calling every elder in the middle of the night, demanding they meet him at the church immediately. I don't know how he got away with it, but they met with him, listened to him, and did what he asked. I think they were afraid not to. Unfortunately, I knew how they felt.

I found it hard to explain such irrational behavior. I did not want to admit to myself that I had made a mistake in marrying Greg. I had learned early on in life that you should not cause problems for the pastor, whether he was your father or your husband. So I moved deeper into denial, not wanting to admit that our problems were serious. I had to protect us from detection and keep anyone from suspecting that we were not the godly Christian family everyone saw on Sunday morning.

Greg often attacked me verbally when I made a mistake or crossed him, until I felt like the most stupid, thoughtless person who ever lived. If I started to cry he would say, "I can't talk to you because all you do is cry."

The verbal abuse over any mistake I made would become so intense that I would often explode emotionally and start screaming or throwing things. Then I would be punished even more by reminders from Greg that he couldn't talk about issues with someone so unstable. He claimed it was always my fault, and I saw myself this way as well. *If I could just do better, we would have a good marriage, and Greg would not be angry,* I reasoned. *I just need to try harder not to upset him.*

Why didn't I stand up to Greg? Why didn't I fight back? Why didn't I refuse to let the temper tantrums control every situation? I have asked myself those questions hundreds of times. I think part of the answer is found in my family background. I was only expected to express good feelings and to keep quiet about bad feelings. Bad feelings, such as anger or frustration, were not Christian. I stuffed them down inside and kept on being the exemplary pastor's daughter. I perpetuated this image as a married woman. Fear kept me from standing up to Greg, but so did my learned behavior from the past. I just couldn't rock the boat.

Of course, there were good times in our marriage. When life was going smoothly, I told myself, hopefully, the temper episodes were in the past and wouldn't happen anymore. When they did, I resigned myself to this way of life in our marriage.

Another move from the country back to a city church and the birth of our third daughter, Kari, kept both of us busy in separate worlds. Greg spent every day at the church office or out with people. Most of my days were occupied caring for three little ones and keeping a home. I didn't mind that Greg was so busy. It was much less stressful in our home when he wasn't there.

Yvonne:

We were enjoying small-town life in our country pastorate. Our daughters, in kindergarten and first grade, had adjusted well to school and friends. Our church was growing, not just in numbers but also spiritually. As we ministered, Ted increasingly found people coming to him for help, especially women. I soon became concerned when women in bad marriages spent more frequent times in counseling. I felt comfortable with the women who came to me, and I found that many trusted me. However, I felt very alarmed when I would hear: "Pastor Ted is so wonderful. I wish I had a husband who treated me like he treats me." Or, "I just know our marriage would be great if only my husband knew the Lord."

Women who saw my husband as the answer to their problems began to irritate me, but I felt guilty for feeling this way. I often expressed my concern to Ted, and he always assured me that he was just being a help. I was particularly concerned about one woman.

One day, as Ted and I were enjoying a game of ping-pong, I dared to ask, "Are you in love with Becky?"

I will never forget the look that crossed his face. He threw down his paddle and spoke in a voice of disbelief. "Yvonne, how could you ask such a thing?"

Not even realizing that he had not answered, I apologized for distrusting him. Then I told him I was worried over the amount of time he spent counseling her.

"Ted, it could be dangerous. Do you realize that Becky is vulnerable to any form of attention? I don't trust her with you. When she tells me how wonderful it must be to be married to you, it makes me sick. Can you understand that?"

Ted assured me that he would be extra careful and observant. He affirmed his love for me, and I felt comforted. "Yvonne, I promise you, if I sense any inappropriate vibes coming from Becky—or any other woman—I will let you know. I'll be careful." He asked me to work with him when he dealt with those in marriage difficulties. Naïvely, I believed him, at least temporarily.

Within the month, Ted and I were discussing the same situation. The queasiness in my stomach had returned and my distrust was building. I would observe hushed conversations. I would see Becky's car parked at the church much more frequently than seemed normal. When I would walk to the church and go in, it all looked innocent, but I no longer believed it.

Finally, Ted admitted to emotional attachment for Becky. She admitted the same. He told me the feelings were there, but he would continue to keep them under control. The day came when I was playing the organ for a wedding, Becky was singing, and Ted was doing the ceremony. I could not keep my mind on the music as I watched the two of them moving around, getting ready for the wedding. I began to realize how ludicrous this all was. I would either have to trust him or find out what was going on.

After the wedding and the reception, I noticed neither Ted nor Becky was present. I wandered from classroom to classroom in the church, then opened a door and found them embracing and kissing one another. Frantically I rushed across the room, grabbed Ted, and pulled him from the embrace. I attacked Becky, hitting her and scratching her face. Ted pulled me off her and held me, not to stop the fight as much as to protect her. My heart pounded in my chest.

Today I laugh, thinking how ridiculous I must have looked. If I really wanted to pound on someone, why wasn't it Ted? Why the "other woman"? The humor escaped me that day. Becky cowered. I shook with anger, but Ted showed no remorse. The scene ended abruptly as our daughters, looking for their parents, wandered in. Pretending as if nothing was wrong, I took them home. It was late at night before I finally went to bed.

Within the hour, Ted came home and crawled in beside me. He took me in his arms and told me he had written a letter of resignation to the church. He stated that he wanted to continue with his schooling. He told me we would move across country. He needed to be out of ministry until he could get right with God and heal our marriage. Again, he only admitted to an emotional attachment, even though I eventually found out that he and Becky had had a full-blown affair.

I believed that marriage is sacred and permanent. I believed that we could rebuild our relationship. I believed that Ted's resignation and his choice to stay out of ministry were signs he wanted to work through his problems. He did tell me that he no longer loved me—he was in love with Becky. I replied that love is action and often misunderstood in the light of passion. I also believed he would again love me, and I set out to be the best wife I could be.

We moved across the country and lived with my sister for a few months. Ted found work, and we found a place to live. We knew it was temporary, and we treated it as such.

I asked two things of Ted. First, that he would ask God every day to restore love for me. Though he thought this was ridiculous—no one can just decide to love—he did make that request daily. He told me he could do that much for me. Second, there would be no further contact with Becky. Though he promised, I still checked up on him. I discovered he had a post office box, where he could receive correspondence without my knowing it (I had discovered letters in his desk at work). I confronted him with the truth and asked that he drop the box. I contacted Becky and told her not to write again. I told both of them I would expose the contact if it did not stop. To my knowledge, that was the last contact between them until many years after we were divorced.

Slowly we rebuilt our relationship. I sensed that Ted did not want to love me. Yet day by day over the months I felt a softening on his part.

"I'm discovering that I can't ask God for love toward you—even when I'm less than genuine—without sensing the old feelings," Ted said.

He often called God the "Hound of Heaven." My heart was warmed, yet I remained cautious. I had been burned before, and I no longer knew how much I could trust this man. God was answering Ted's prayer in spite of himself. Or maybe God was answering my daily prayer for the same thing. In any case, God seemed to be doing a work in his heart.

Thank you, Lord! Before long we had a group of friends who wanted us to hold a Bible study in their home. Ted was skilled at this type of interaction and eventually agreed to lead the study. He thrived on ministry to individuals and did a great job. Our new friends knew no details about why we were not in ministry at this time, and we never talked about it. Ted wanted me to accompany him to these studies. Hope sprang up in my heart, and I realized this was a healthy sign for our marriage.

This Bible study brought back our passion for ministry. Ted and I talked long about his desires. Had he negated his call to ministry by marital infidelity? If he could rebuild his marriage, could God still use him as a pastor? If he did take a church, should he be completely honest with them? Would it be enough to answer all questions honestly but not offer unsolicited information? If God forgives and cleanses, does he not also restore?

We talked about God's promise to his people in the book of Joel. Though the land had been destroyed by plague and locusts, God promised that their repentance would result in his restoring the years that the locusts had eaten. Could God restore what the locusts had eaten in our lives? We believed he could.

We did not solicit information about churches looking for a pastor. We prayed and asked God to open doors if he wanted us back in ministry. Then a call came from a pastor across the country. "There is a small country church near me that is looking for a pastor. Are you interested? Would it be okay if I give them your names?"

Could this be an open door? It was near Ted's family. Our emotions ran wild as we talked with excitement about the possibilities. We loved the country church we had been in, so this church appealed to us. We had never lived close to Ted's family. Finally our girls would get to know grandparents they had seen only a few times. Both of us felt this was a door we should walk through. We agreed to be completely honest with the church board concerning any questions they asked us. We knew our answers could deny us the position, but we placed everything in God's hands. We did, however, agree to say nothing about what we were *not* asked. At the time we did not view this as deceptive.

When we arrived at our new home, the four of us felt a sense of relief. We were home. Even the cat sensed our ease and settled in. We spent the next six years there with wonderful ministry and wonderful memories.

Or so I thought.

Joanne and Yvonne:

Often when Yvonne and I talked over the past, we would ask each other, "Were we that naïve? What about our dreams?" We had believed that marriage, family, and ministry were all a part of who we were, and they would continue. As the dreams began to crumble, we believed we could make it through and rebuild any damage. And for a while, we did.

Were our dreams wrong? No.

Dreams about a godly spouse, great family life, and ministry to other people were very much what God wanted in our lives. These were our motivation for living. Jesus Christ tells us that he not only came to give us life, but also to give it "more abundantly." Life, at its best, was supposed to be this way—wasn't it? Without a dream, where would be the sense of future or ambition to accomplish a goal? We believe that Greg and Ted mutually shared our dreams.

Were all our dreams realistic? Not completely.

In retrospect, both of us realized we entered marriage believing we could control much more of it than was possible. It wasn't that we wanted to be "in control" as much as we both believed if we were the best wives possible, God would honor our motives and bless us. The reality is, you can't be responsible for your mate, nor can you change the other person. Each of us stands before God and is accountable to him. Nor can you expect your spouse to fit into your dreams the way "Ken" would do for "Barbie."

There is something good about the old expression, "Love is blind." Loving someone helps us live with a spouse's idiosyncrasies that others would find intolerable. Yet loving someone can also cause blindness to deception. Yvonne and I wanted to believe in a fairy-tale love, and so we were too often blind to reality.

In that familiar passage on love, in 1 Corinthians 13, we read that "[love] does not hold grudges and will hardly even notice when others do it wrong. It is never glad about injustice, but rejoices whenever truth wins out. If you love someone you will be loyal to him no matter what the cost. You will always believe in him, always expect the best of him, and always stand your ground in defending him" (verses 5–7 TLB). These are great attributes. But truth is distorted when a spouse wants to believe that everything is okay and lives in denial.

There came a point when both Yvonne and I realized that the loss of our dreams was not our fault. It was a revelation to us because we had played the role of being responsible for everything that happened. In both of our cases, we were the glue that kept the family together. But at what cost? We were about to find out.

I (Joanne) tended to be a people pleaser, willing to let the other person lead. I had learned this behavior pattern while growing up, and I could easily play the passive wife. However, I lived in a world of fear I had never before experienced. Greg's frequent bouts of anger controlled me in a way I had not known in my quiet childhood. Now I often faced days when I walked on eggshells to avoid conflict. My goal was to be the best wife I could be so as not to upset Greg. I became responsible for keeping peace in the home so that he could concentrate on his work. Any deviation made me a target for his anger. I worked hard to maintain the image of the Christian family.

I didn't realize the lack of freedom I was experiencing. Yes, I often felt like a caged animal, but I had no idea I was building my own cage. My bondage was because I allowed it. Would things have been different if I had stood up to this man early in our marriage rather than enduring his anger for more than twenty-five years? I will never know.

The one area of my life that I could control was my home. I became obsessive about keeping my house in order, my children dressed neatly, and every dresser drawer organized. There was no clutter in my home, only internal chaos in me.

Yvonne's marriage, however, was reasonably calm. She and Ted lived in comparative harmony. When there was a fight, it was often about the lack of time Ted spent at home with her and the children. She was usually the initiator of this debate, pursuing the conversation and asking for time. Ted seldom reacted, except to explain the temporary situation.

"When you stack a temporary upon a temporary upon a temporary, it becomes a permanent," she replied. Then she would feel guilty for starting the argument, and the guilt drove deeper into her soul when she realized her demands were keeping him from his ministry. So she would back up, regroup, and try to be the best wife possible. She believed her expectations of time and commitment were realistic, but couldn't help feeling that she was being unfair.

In retrospect, Yvonne experienced false guilt. Her real struggle was sorting out truth in Ted's dealings with women. There were many times she felt uneasy about banter and flirtatious talk between Ted and teens in the youth group or some woman in the congregation. She would seldom say anything because he would invalidate her concerns. Could these be danger signs for infidelity in marriage? Was her "woman's intuition" picking up what she could never admit? She came to believe that she was being paranoid and tried not to be jealous.

It is appropriate to expect faithfulness in marriage. In fact, when Paul lists the qualities of a leader, he states that a deacon should be the husband of one wife (1 Tim. 3:2). These words mean his loyalty should be to one woman—alone. A leader should be accountable to someone, and he should be loyal to his wife. The vows of fidelity and loyalty are paramount in a marriage.

Our shared dream was fading, yet we lived on in these relationships. The job now was to do the right thing so that life would go as smoothly as possible. At least there would be an image of a good family. We would maintain home life and dedicate ourselves to the task.

I lived from day to day, hoping Greg would not flare up. Many days were good. When life turned for the worse, I waited for the storm to calm, continuing to bury my anger deep inside.

Yvonne and Ted rebuilt their relationship and had several good years. There were no affairs—or at least none that she knew about. The ironic thing about a spouse having an affair is that it is hard to know if he or she is being faithful later. But she believed, not only because there seemed to be no evidence but also because she wanted to believe. Years later, when there was evidence again, the re-created dream was replaced by harsh reality.

What if we had opened our eyes to the real men we had married? Who was the real person? We are all capable of disobedience to God in so many ways. No one is perfect. So where do we draw our boundaries for those with whom we live?

Healthy family members hold each other accountable. They communicate and work together for each other's good and the good of the family. Sadly, this was lost in Greg's and Ted's choices to put self-gratification above individual healthiness and family wholeness.

One day, Yvonne and I were eating breakfast at a restaurant. We discussed the role of a wife in confronting her husband over issues that concern her. I shared insight from a friend.

"Do you remember John Walsh? He said he had discovered that men in general don't want to take on guilt or blame, especially from their wives. So what is the wife's appropriate role?"

"John's opinion makes sense," Yvonne sighed as a crooked smile crossed her lips. "It may not be fair, but it makes sense. Ted once told me that he had enough trouble with his one conscience. He didn't need two!"

We both agreed that in a good relationship it is appropriate to "speak the truth in love" (Eph. 4:15a). A wife should not be afraid to do so. However, the truth often is more palatable coming from a good friend rather than a spouse. This is a great reason for any believer to have an accountability partner.

Women often find another woman to talk with and seek advice from. Yvonne and I do this for each other. Proverbs states, "As iron sharpens iron, so a man sharpens the countenance of his friend" (Prov. 27:17

NKJV). Fewer men have accountability partners. However, it is a great idea. We are seeing more personal accountability in churches today as men share their deepest struggles with other men.

All marriages have their problems. All good marriages take work and time commitment. Families in ministry are especially vulnerable. Satan is on the attack. If he can destroy the pastoral family, he can bring down many other families as well. The busyness of the ministry often takes priority over the mundane issues of family, so the urgent overrides the important.

Keeping up an image of a functioning family seems important. People are watching. Those in leadership are expected to be examples for other believers. Paul exhorts the young pastor, Timothy, to "be an example to the believers in word, in conduct [conversation], in love, in spirit, in faith, in purity. Till I come, give attention to reading, to exhortation, to doctrine" (1 Tim. 4:12–13 NKJV).

So where is the line drawn between being genuine and "airing dirty laundry"? Pretense and deception are never helpful. Living lives of integrity is. Were we guilty of lying to ourselves and to others? Did we set in place a covering of pretense that would drag us further into deception? We had good times and good years. But there would be more lies, more cover up, and more destruction. Would we survive the next onslaught?

CHAPTER 4

Are You Having an Affair?

Covering the truth to pacify me

Joanne:

I stared at this woman with growing apprehension. What should I say to her? Her tall, slim body was wrapped in a beautiful robe of shimmering rose-colored silk. She paced the floor nervously, continually running her fingers through her shoulder-length, blonde hair. I'd never been this close to a real actress before. Next to her, I was suddenly very conscious of my dull, tired, mother-of-four-small-children harassed appearance. This lady had lived a glamorous Hollywood life. True, she had only bit parts in movies and commercials, but still . . .

Four years earlier we had moved again, and Greg was now senior pastor of a growing church. We had come filled with excitement to this small church. We found warm, loving folks who helped us settle into our modest ranch-style house. The Friday night before our first Sunday, the congregation held a reception for us with welcoming speeches and a beautifully decorated cake that said, *Welcome to our new pastor and family!*

I was so hopeful that this would be a new beginning for us. Greg was full of plans and ideas for ministering to this group that seemed so ready for anything he could offer.

Two years later, our fourth daughter, Alexi, was born. I was busy at home, taking care of four children, and Greg seemed to be thriving on an overloaded schedule of having meetings, doing home Bible studies, counseling, preaching, and planning church events. The church was growing quite rapidly, and a committee had started looking for property on which to construct a new building. Greg was pouring all his energies into a growing church. As he became immersed in the work, his time at home became scarce. I didn't mind because the stress level in the home was also lowered.

Now I stood facing this woman who lit one cigarette after another and continued to pace up and down the length of her hospital room. It was hospital policy in that area to call a pastor when a patient had written on admittance papers that he or she had no church connection but desired to have a pastor visit. This woman had been admitted to the psychiatric floor of the hospital with severe depression.

Earlier in the day Greg had called me from his office: "Joanne, I just got a call from the hospital. There's a patient asking for a pastor to visit her. She's had some kind of emotional breakdown. I can't possibly get there today; do you think you could go?"

"What would I say to her?" I blurted out, feeling very inadequate.

"Just be friendly and get acquainted with her. You don't have to say anything profound. Tell her who you are, and explain that I couldn't come today but will come in the next day or two. You don't even have to stay long."

I thought about all I would have to do—shower and change clothes, then try to find a babysitter. But this was a chance to be involved in ministry, so I agreed to do it. I called Ruth, an older woman in the church who lived alone and often volunteered to take care of the girls for me. She was like a grandmother to them, and they loved her. I readied myself quickly, bundled all four girls into the car, drove them to Ruth's, and then went on to the hospital.

That was how I met Vicki. I didn't stay long, and although she was polite, I came away feeling she was very disappointed to see me and not my husband. She didn't have to be disappointed long. Greg visited her a few days later and was soon seeing her often. When she was released from the hospital, he encouraged her to start coming to church, where she would find supportive friends. She came and seemed genuine in getting acquainted with people, but it was Greg she depended on when she got depressed.

I began to notice that when Vicki was around, Greg would joke with her, tease her, and act as though there was something special between them. I dismissed my fears that something might be going on. I needed to have faith in our marriage, regardless of past troubles. *After all, my husband was the pastor of a church that had grown to 800 people,* I thought. *He wouldn't do anything to jeopardize his success!* I trusted him, even in the face of growing suspicions.

Vicki invited us to a party at her house one night. Her parents were visiting, and she wanted us to meet them—at least that's what she said. In reality, it was just an excuse to spend an evening with my husband, as events of the night soon revealed. She greeted us at the door, and after a brief nod to me, she took Greg's arm and led him over to her parents to be introduced as *her* pastor. I felt invisible and ignored, but I didn't blame Greg. I was quite sure I knew what Vicki was doing, but I trusted my husband.

At the end of the evening she had someone take a picture of Greg and her. That did it! I was hurt and angry. As soon as we got in the car to go home, I confronted him. "Greg, how could you let her do that to me? She may not have wanted me in the picture, but you sure could've included me. That was very embarrassing. She made it obvious to everyone there how she feels about you."

I lapsed into silence, wanting to hear him acknowledge how badly Vicki had acted and to come to my defense. Instead, he brushed off my questions with vague answers about Vicki being a very needy person and a new Christian. *We* needed to be patient with her. I was terribly hurt by his defense of her, but chose to bury it.

A few weeks later, Vicki stopped speaking to me. If I saw her at church and said, "Hi," she looked past me or turned away. I told Greg what she was doing, but he defended her. "She's struggling with many problems and needs our patience."

He always made me feel as though I was wrong whenever I was upset, but I knew I had a right to question her behavior. His comments hurt; I wanted him to feel the same as I did. I needed to know that he would not let this woman break into the privacy of our marriage. But I was too reluctant and afraid to look at what might be happening, so I just threw this problem under the bed with all the other monsters that threatened to destroy us.

Even when an older, mature Christian came to me and asked what was going on between Greg and Vicki, I just smiled and said, "Nothing, Ken. Vicki is a hurting, needy woman, but I trust my husband."

I used the very words that Greg had said to me, although deep inside I knew they were not true.

He frowned and shook his head. "I hope you are right, for your sake."

I didn't feel I convinced him. He had noticed Greg once before in a similar situation and voiced the same concern to me.

The real story of Greg and Vicki's relationship began to surface after Greg returned from a two-day pastors' conference in a city eighty miles away. I asked him about the conference, and he didn't give me any details. He just said it had been good and he needed to get back to work. He didn't seem like himself. He was quiet and subdued. I figured he was tired from the trip and all the meetings.

A few days later, he came home from the church office unexpectedly at noon. I was surprised to see him. He usually filled his days with appointments, planning sessions, studying, and counseling, and wasn't home until dinnertime. He was very agitated. Before I had a chance to ask him anything, he blurted out, "You have to come with me to the office. Vicki told Dave and Stacy that she and I are having an affair. They are very upset. They insist on meeting with me and two of the elders. I need you there."

My heart started pounding. Yet I felt almost relieved that now we could be honest with each other because this was out in the open. I looked directly at my husband and said, "Before I go anywhere with you, I need to know the truth. Are you having an affair with Vicki?"

His reply was terse. "Of course I'm not. She's making it up. She's a disturbed person."

I believed him, choosing to do so because I needed to keep my world together for the sake of the family and the church. I went to the meeting with him and sat by his side, facing a visibly upset young couple and two concerned elders. When Dave and Stacy related what Vicki had told them and fired their questions at Greg, his denial of any romantic involvement with Vicki sounded so convincing. He was the pastor, in control of this meeting, assuring everyone her accusations were not true, and she was, after all, still struggling with serious depression.

I added to this assurance by defending him. I even talked about the good marriage we had and said that maybe Vicki was jealous. My statements seemed to convince everyone that Greg had spoken the truth. After all, if a wife is sure of her husband's fidelity, it must be so. Actually, I think everyone wanted to believe Greg.

Greg had been a great encouragement to Dave and Stacy in their spiritual growth, and they loved him. The elders were excited and happy over the way the church was thriving. Who would want to see that end? Greg taught truth from the pulpit; why wouldn't he speak truth now? Vicki's accusations didn't stand a chance.

The meeting ended with prayer, hugs, and handshakes all around. Everyone seemed very relieved, especially Greg. We didn't talk much on the way home. Greg's mind was already focused on the next day's activities. That was typical behavior. Unpleasant situations were never discussed again. But putting unresolved issues on a shelf did not help our marriage. I was stuffing all these issues inside and distancing myself from my husband.

As the church continued to grew, Greg asked the board to hire an associate pastor. They agreed we needed one and left it up to Greg to bring someone in for their approval. He chose Scott, a very strong-minded, charismatic man who had been in the business world before deciding to enter seminary and ministry. Several of his references had advised against hiring him as an associate, claiming he was better suited as a senior pastor. Greg's pride in his success with a fast-growing ministry caused him to see this as a challenge. With the church's approval, Scott joined the staff.

It didn't take long for Greg and Scott to start disagreeing. Scott began to challenge Greg on things he observed that puzzled him. Greg saw these challenges as personal affronts and grew defensive. The situation became so tense after about a year that the board asked both of them to get some counseling before the church split. People were aware of their struggles, and some sided with Scott.

Greg and I left early on a Monday morning for a three-hour drive to visit our friend and mentor, Pastor Ed Thomas. As we pulled into the driveway Greg said to me, "There's something I need to tell you before we go in." He shut off the engine, and looking straight ahead, blurted out, "I know Pastor Ed is going to ask me if I'm involved with another woman. He's always warning me about counseling women without someone else present. I will have to tell him this, so I'm telling you first."

The wall of denial that protected my world, my dreams, and my self-made way of life began to crumble as reality forced its way into my unwilling mind. *I know what you're going to say; I've known it all along.*

Greg continued. "Do you remember the pastors' conference last month? Well, I didn't go to the conference. I met Vicki at a motel and stayed overnight with her. We didn't have sex, but we slept together, and she tried to get me to run away with her. I refused to go, and I think that's why she told people we were having an affair. She was angry with me."

He stopped talking, and I sat in numb silence. All I could think of was that our wedding vows were nothing but empty words. I felt as though the privacy of our marriage—and my heart—had been ripped open, exposed and trampled on. His "no sex" declaration was ludicrous. Did he really expect me to believe that? He had lied about this whole affair. Why should I believe him now? With a sinking heart, I determined that I would never again believe anything he said. I wondered if he even knew how to tell the truth. How many other lies had he told me? Did I know him at all?

There were no apologies or pleas for forgiveness. Greg acted as if he was frustrated because he knew this had to come out in the open. He also talked as though he hadn't done anything wrong, because after all, "he hadn't run off with her and they hadn't had sex." He was so absorbed in himself that he was oblivious to my pain.

We got out of the car and went inside. I kept thinking I should be a hysterical mess by now, but I had stuffed my emotions for far too long.

The session with Pastor Ed went exactly as Greg had predicted. His first question to Greg was, "Are you involved with another woman?" As Pastor Ed probed, Greg confessed that the meetings he was supposedly at in the evenings were actually spent at Vicki's apartment. But he insisted he was just "helping her spiritually." He also attempted to explain the motel weekend. Pastor Ed frowned at Greg's declaration of innocence.

"Greg, quit rationalizing! You're trying to justify yourself, but your disloyalty to Joanne is the real issue."

The conflict with Greg's associate was set aside as Pastor Ed tried to impress on Greg the need for counseling for both of us. He pointed out the damage done and said this could not be resolved in one afternoon. He strongly suggested we stay overnight and continue to talk tomorrow. He offered to set aside his own schedule for the next day and spend it with us, but Greg refused to stay, saying that he had to return home because of his own schedule. It amazed me to hear him talk about his work as if nothing had happened. In my mind I expected the whole world to stop while we dealt with this crisis.

We left late that night. On the way home, I questioned Greg several times concerning his relationship with Vicki.

"I don't want to talk about it! I'm tired, and we can talk later," he said.

We never did talk. If I brought up the subject he would glare at me. "I told you everything there is to tell. Drop it!" Then he would throw out Paul's admonition to "forget the past and press forward." I've tried to understand why Greg responds to crises by isolating each incidence so that he doesn't have to acknowledge it happened. Some counselors suggest that in time he may very well believe these incidences really didn't happen.

Greg acted as if this affair never happened. No one in the church knew about it. Vicki went to live in Colorado. I stuffed more anger and pain inside. I performed beautifully as the pastor's wife. I taught Bible classes and Sunday school classes and had people over for dinner on Sundays and even helped Greg teach some marriage seminars. Inside I was screaming for help, but who would help me? I was afraid to tell my parents anything; it would hurt them too much. I could not talk to anyone at church—that would be unfair to Greg.

The conflicts with Scott increased and finally came to a head. It was evident to the elders that they needed to bring this situation before the congregation. When I walked into the meeting, the air was thick with tension. But it was nothing compared to my inner turmoil.

Both Scott and Greg were given an opportunity to speak. I listened to Greg justify himself and act as though he had offered Scott a share in every part of the ministry but Scott had betrayed him. I knew this wasn't true, and I felt nauseated. When the elders decided that Scott would have to resign, I couldn't listen anymore. I walked out of the meeting, determined that I would no longer take part in this awful charade. I could not go on pretending.

Later that week I went to some friends of ours, Mike and Michelle, and told them how Greg controlled the family with his anger, how hard he had been on Scott, and that he had not been truthful in the business meeting. I told them that he had lied about his relationship with Vicki, and I could not go on living with him as long as all these things stood between us. They advised me to tell Greg we had talked and to ask him to come back to their house.

I went back, but as I approached the house my heart was pounding with fear. *How far can I push him before he becomes completely irrational and even physically abusive? Why would he listen now when he has never listened before?* My fears were justified. Before I had two sentences out of my mouth, he started yelling obscene words at me and to stormed out of the house. The tires squealed as the car roared out of the driveway.

The girls' faces were white with fear; they had witnessed the whole scene. They huddled in a little group and looked at me, waiting for some word that would restore their world. Eight-year-old Alexi started to cry. "Why are you and Daddy fighting?" she sobbed.

I just drew her close and hugged her. I had no comforting words. I was living in unbelievable stress, trying to decide what to do. There is no way to describe the desperation that drove me to this point. I was at the end of my endurance, and I knew it. My concern for the church, the girls, Scott and his family, and our marriage had me spiraling down into a dark hole.

I hugged the girls and told them I was going to get some help for all of us. Then I called a friend who had several children the same ages as the girls.

"Cathy, I can't explain anything right now. I need you to keep the girls for me, and I'll tell you what's going on as soon as I can." Fortunately she didn't ask any questions.

"Send them over and don't worry; they can stay as long as needed." Their house was just a block away, so I let the girls walk.

As soon as they were gone, I called Michelle. Words tumbled out of my mouth.

"Michelle, come get me out of this house. I can't stay here right now. I'm afraid Greg will come back, and I don't know what he'll do."

I threw some clothes in a bag and waited anxiously by the front door, hoping Michelle would arrive before Greg. The empty house was dark and foreboding, the air heavy. Anxiety choked my breathing. I had no idea what I was going to do. I just needed to get away from the guise of normalcy I had so carefully built there.

Overwhelming grief filled me, due to the pain and anxiety I saw on my children's faces. Frantic questions raced through my mind. *How would I take care of them? How could I explain my actions? God, where are you? Why is this happening to us? Was I wrong to expose the truth?*

I spent the next few days at Michelle's house. I couldn't sleep, I couldn't eat, and I couldn't stop crying. My emotions were in complete turmoil, and I felt smothered in guilt over my broken family. But I felt tremendous relief in not having to cover up and pretend anymore. *Where would we go from here? What would the church do about our situation?*

Yvonne:

"Are you in love with Becky?" I remembered asking that question years earlier.

"Yvonne, how could you ask such a thing?" He made me feel I should never have asked.

This conversation was coming back to haunt me, but now I was far less gullible.

Ted and I had been at our country church for six years, our second pastorate. Ted's schedule was busy enough that the urgent often took precedence over the important, giving him limited time with the family. Yet I believed our marriage was healthy. When we did have time together, it was usually fun. When there were arguments between us, they were mostly about time commitments and his lack of making me a priority. I was the one who complained—sometimes nagged—for more of his time. Then I would feel guilty for taking him away from ministry.

The girls were now teenagers and part of a great youth group. They seemed to fit in well and had many friends. They even got along with each other. During these years, on numerous occasions we had other children living with us because they needed a stable environment.

I had done well at trusting the man I married. I had kept him accountable after the affair with Becky several years before. I knew there were many couples who had gone through these kinds of marital difficulties and who now lived in restored relationships. I had witnessed situations in which the wife had been betrayed by infidelity and was never able to trust again. That lack of trust destroyed the marriage. I determined that I would not be that woman, and I asked God for strength to be the wife he wanted me to be.

In spite of what had happened, I still chose to believe in Ted. We talked about his love for counseling. We determined as a couple that he would always use me in the counseling process when dealing with vulnerable women. Ted often requested that we talk over issues. This made me feel needed and useful. I was reassured that he understood his vulnerability and was allowing me to fill a much-needed role. I believed that he was being honest with me.

However, as life got busier I began to feel left out of conversations. Ted would leave the house and be gone for hours, with no explanation of his whereabouts. When I talked to him, he seemed distant and uninterested. He even seemed uninterested in sex, which was unusual. For a while I suspected he was too busy and too tired. It appeared he was cutting himself off from me, not others. He seemed to have very close relationships with a few women.

Since Ted's office was in our home, I knew who he was counseling, but I noticed he had stopped including me. Concerned, I decided to confront him.

"Ted, I need to talk to you. I thought we had an agreement, an agreement that you would not see vulnerable women by yourself."

He leaned back in his chair, gazing out the window for a few moments. Then he looked me in the eye and stated matter-of-factly, "Well, yes, but I don't know what your problem is. Don't you trust me?"

Is he playing me for a fool? Old memories resurfaced.

"We also had an agreement that you would trust my instincts over your own. It's that woman's intuition thing, you know. If I feel suspicious, maybe there's something there."

"Yvonne, there's nothing," Ted continued defensively. "Don't be so paranoid."

My stomach lurched as I wiped my sweaty palms across my jeans. *Could I be paranoid? Just because I am paranoid, does that mean there isn't any reason for it?* I chose my words carefully now, but I knew my tone of voice carried an edge.

"I'm not comfortable with the amount of time you're spending counseling. I'm not comfortable with the particular women you see."

Ted's voice sounded guarded. "You can't be serious. I always include you, especially when it involves marriage issues."

"I'm not certain that's true. You only include me when it's obvious to both of us. I don't think you're being honest with me or, for that matter, honest with yourself."

I could see the conversation was going nowhere. Every time I voiced concern, he reassured me that there was nothing to worry about.

I'm starting to sound like a nag, I thought. *I'm sure that's how he perceives me.* Yet, I couldn't get rid of the queasiness in my stomach. Finally, in desperation, I asked the question I had hoped I would never have to ask again.

"Are you having an affair?"

He looked at me and with no hesitation said, "No, I'm not having an affair!" Then he defied me. "But if I were, you know I could look you straight in the eye and deny it!"

I suddenly realized that, yes, he would lie to me if he were having an affair. He was becoming an expert at telling me what I wanted to hear. This was deliberate deception, with the intent to divert me.

The next few days were a jumble of confusion. I set out to separate truth from lies. Normally we could communicate reasonably well, but this conversation had unnerved me. I was convinced his evasiveness was a cover-up for an affair. I discovered that by putting a glass to the floor in the bedroom above Ted's office I could hear snatches of his phone conversations. I looked in his office desk drawers for notes. I watched his every move. I was becoming what I never wanted to be—and I was justifying it! By the time I had enough evidence that Ted could not discount it, he began to tell me enough to appease me. Though there were affairs with three women over a period of a few months, he told me as little as he could to lessen my current suspicion.

Ted explained his affair with the first woman. He told me that Sally had repeatedly made passes at him and suggested she enticed him into the relationship. He explained, with apparent remorse, that he gave in to her continual pressure and had sex one time with her. He told me that he felt awful afterwards and wanted nothing (physically) to do with her again.

I believed his story that Sally was the initiator because I wanted to. It made me feel better about myself to blame the "other woman." Just as I had attacked Becky years earlier, I could now direct my feelings toward Sally. I admitted to myself, however, that Ted could have made different choices.

His story moved to the affair with the second woman. Ted told me that since he had already yielded to sexual desires and "messed up," it made little difference whether or not he was in another affair.

That's twisted, I thought. *Satan's old lie: "Only once will not hurt." Then, after it's done: "You've blown it now, so what's the difference?"*

I listened in disbelief as Ted continued his justification. He really liked Delores, but had been cold and distant to her for some time. She was offended and confronted him on his behavior. He told her his distance had been because he had strong emotional feelings for her. Delores, married to a man who gave her little time and romance, was vulnerable and ready for such a message. So began the affair, which lasted a few months.

I could no longer blame the "other woman." This was Ted's pursuit.

"How could you go to her and let her know your feelings? That's stupid, just plain stupid! You knew her vulnerability. You knew she'd be putty in your hands. You're sick!" My lip was quivering. I was losing control. I felt betrayed by my husband and a woman who had been a close friend.

Ted confessed to me that he had struggled with his infidelity and decided to end the affair. I was in turmoil, having no idea where to go from here. I knew it was possible to rebuild a marriage after unfaithfulness. We had done so. I also knew that, short of a miracle of God, I would not be as trusting again.

Life went on from day to day, mostly because I didn't know what to do or where to draw the line. *These affairs were over, weren't they? What was I supposed to do?* We needed help.

I became more passionate and aggressive in our love making. I was out to prove something to Ted—and to myself—that I really was desirable. I recalled that Ted and I had a book (*Sex Begins in the Kitchen* by Kevin Lehman),[1] which we intended to read together. I looked for the book and discovered it was missing. Ted said he had given it to Delores.

"Get it back now!" I was furious and insulted that he wouldn't have time to read it with me but would give it to Delores to read. A few days later he handed me the book. Carefully and deliberately, I started to tear it into strips. He just stood and watched me for several minutes, until the whole book was shredded. Neither of us said a word, and then he left the room.

Delores knew that Ted had told me about their affair. We were friends, and she came to me, asking for my forgiveness. After a long and tearful conversation, we hugged each other. I told her I chose to forgive her. I was able to do this for two reasons. First, I had carefully studied Christ's forgiveness for me when I had needed to work through forgiveness issues in the past. I had begun to understand grace when I needed to show grace. Second, I could see clearly who my husband had become—or always was. I no longer looked at him through rose-colored glasses. I knew that he preyed on vulnerable women and used this vulnerability to his advantage.

I could now define his behavior as abusive towards women. I could place the blame squarely where it belonged—on the one God had placed in leadership. Ted had misused his authority. He was not a shepherd; he was a deceiver.

"Yvonne, why do you think Ted told you about us? What motivated him?" Delores asked.

This question made no sense. Confused, I tried to explain how our conversation had gone. "Obviously, Ted didn't want to tell me. He struggled with it, but decided he needed to come clean with me."

"Open your eyes, Yvonne!" Delores demanded. "He would never have told you about us unless he was trying to divert your attention."

Realization swept over me. Ted's truth twisting had deceived me again. I would have to sort through everything he had told me with suspicion. *Of course the affair with Delores was over, because he had moved on to someone else.* Delores and I talked about the possibility that their affair would still be happening except that now there was a new person on the scene. I instinctively knew who this third woman was, even before Delores confirmed it. I had seen evidence of someone Ted was "helping" with struggles. Patty was a beautiful woman, married, with children. She began sharing some of her pain with Ted. In his state of mind, this was a new challenge. Because Patty was so vulnerable, the conquest happened quickly.

I was reasonably young, but no longer innocent. I couldn't believe anything this man said to me. *How gullible does he think I am? It would be so easy to become cynical. Can I trust anyone ever again?*

The deception followed as Ted and Patty secretly made plans to run off together. They connived together to make this arrangement look better. It included the audacity to try to set me up with her husband in a sexual relationship. I was horrified and insulted! I couldn't believe the lengths Ted was willing to go to for his own gratification, yet I realized this was not rational thinking. Aware that he would manipulate anyone in order to get what he wanted, I also knew that he would willingly drag me down to his level in order to feel good about himself.

As far as I knew, our daughters were not aware of the marital turmoil, yet I couldn't help thinking they would soon be confused and wondering what was going on. I had no idea what was to become of our rocky marriage, but I was paralyzed when it came to making any decisions. I didn't believe in divorce, yet our marriage was in serious trouble. I struggled with the fact that Ted had broken our marriage vows, and I believed I had the biblical grounds to legally dissolve this union. Yet I did not have the desire or the strength to take the first step.

It was about this time that Ted told me that he was leaving. The next day he told the girls. They cried but did not appear to be surprised. After their initial tears, Beth showed little emotion and seemed to erect a wall between herself and her father. Had I been more observant, I would have realized she was only adding to the wall that had been there for a couple of years. Anne, on the other hand, seemed to be losing her best friend. She and her father had been buddies forever. She was definitely "Daddy's girl."

Ted told us that he would resign the next Sunday and would give two months' notice. We woke that Sunday morning to the worst blizzard of the winter. There were no plows out, and the snow was still coming down. Churches throughout the area were canceling services, and ours was no exception. For the first time, we had no service, and I wondered about the coincidence. Ted's carefully prepared speech was delayed until the following week. Meanwhile, the girls and I were living in numbness and shock.

In surreal reality, life continued over the next few months. Ted left the house when he felt like it. He would tell me that he was going to see Patty, and I just shrugged. There was no relationship between us. Feeling completely abandoned, I turned to the only One who could give me comfort. It's amazing that we so often don't need God when things are going well, yet when we desperately need him, he is there. I discovered a Friend who would never betray me.

For our daughters, life with Dad became tense, as we all knew he was only biding his time until he left on a plane for his intended destination. We felt as though we were in a pretend world, pretending to be a family.

One incident stands out in my mind. All four of us were in the kitchen getting a snack. Ted started to tell the girls what he wanted them to do. Beth sarcastically retorted, "Who are you to tell me how to behave?" In a rage I had never before seen, he grabbed her, knocked her to the floor, and held her down.

I ran over, took hold of his arm, and pulled him off of her.

"You will never treat your girls like that," I said through clenched teeth. "You will answer to me if you do."

Turning on his heel, he left the room without an apology. We were all in tears. I knew that Beth had lost respect for her father, but I made the assumption that this was about his disloyalty to me. I would soon learn another reason for this strange behavior. The day he left, the girls revealed sickening secrets. I believe this flare-up was an attempt to make certain they didn't tell all they knew.

My marriage was over. My husband of fifteen years was leaving me and the children with no apparent remorse. I had no idea what I would do for a living. I lived in the parsonage and would have to move. All of my family lived more than a thousand miles away. The girls would lose their father, their pastor, their home, their school, their friends, their church, and their youth group in one swoop. And I would have to be there to pick up the pieces.

Joanne and Yvonne:

"Are you having an affair?" It's a question no one wants to ask his or her marriage partner, but we had to ask it.

Is the old adage, "Love is blind," a positive or a negative part of marriage? It can be positive when couples choose to be blind to small irritations. The negative side: It's easier to fool the partner who is committed to trust. Trust means overlooking faults and being vulnerable to pain. I wanted to trust my husband. I (Joanne) chose to believe him rather than the evidence around me or other people's warnings.

C.S. Lewis, in an excerpt from *The Four Loves,* states: "To love at all is to be vulnerable. Love anything, and your heart will certainly be wrung and possibly be broken."[2]

The very act of making vows opens both partners to wounds when the vows are broken. Becoming one flesh is more than physical union. There is a sense in which two people become part of each other emotionally and spiritually. Adultery tears apart that union, causing terrible pain.

I (Joanne) felt betrayed, exposed, and discarded, like a worn-out piece of clothing. These thoughts ran through my head constantly. *Can I ever trust my husband again? Will I be suspicious every time he says he had a meeting or counseling session? Where was he really when he called to say he'd be late for supper? Am I a failure as a sexual partner?*

I struggled for a long time with a sense of failure and inadequacy. I felt God had betrayed me, too. In the months after the first separation, I received many cards from people in the church. Almost every one of them had a verse from the Bible, either printed on the card or handwritten. I threw them away. I also threw away notes from Bible studies I had taught. I was reacting to my hurt and pain. In essence, I was throwing away God. Thank goodness God doesn't throw us away! In the Psalms David says, "You hem me in—behind and before; you have laid your hand upon me. . . . Where can I go from your Spirit? Where can I flee from your presence?" (Ps. 139:5, 7).

God knew exactly what my wounded heart needed, and he provided it. There was one card I didn't throw away. It came from a pastor friend who heard about our tragedy. Respecting his spiritual maturity and wisdom, I opened the card. Sure enough, there was a verse inside, and for some reason my heart latched onto the truth of its words:

> *Because of the LORD's great love we are not consumed,*
> *for his compassions never fail.*
> *They are new every morning; great is your faithfulness.*
> (Lam. 3:22–23)

Consumed? Yes, I felt consumed, over my head in trouble. Compassion? Yes, I needed to feel someone cared about me with great tenderness. Faithful? I needed a faithful God who would never betray me. God drew me back to himself with his words of truth. My emotions did not quiet down all at once, and there were times when I just hung onto those verses with my fingernails to keep from falling into complete despair.

Yvonne found help and comfort in 1 Peter. Initially, verses in the third chapter drew her attention. Peter addresses the wife. He talks about her quiet, hidden beauty of spirit being an inspiration to a husband. Yvonne realized that her spirit had not always been a priority. Sadly, Ted used this new effort on her part to excuse his own behavior. He told their daughter Anne, "If your mom had been this nice to me all along, maybe none of this would have happened. I might have stayed with her."

Yvonne overheard this conversation but decided not to put Anne in the middle of any discussion. Later she confronted Ted. "It's inappropriate to tell Anne what you did. It's too much to ask her to sort out. Even if I had been 'The Wicked Witch of the West,' that doesn't excuse cheating on me. You're trying to justify your wrong behavior and get on Anne's good side. That isn't fair to her or me."

As Yvonne continued to study 1 Peter, she realized most of the book was about suffering. She felt like a martyr, and God spoke to her through the book. She realized that God is honored when we suffer unjustly, Jesus Christ's suffering being the example.

God provided more comfort to her through his words in Proverbs 3:5–8. She knew she had to trust God for the future, since she had no answers. She couldn't depend on her own understanding and needed God to direct her paths. She drew strength from these truths. Her faith in God was confirmed by an act of love. The church people purchased a farewell gift for the family the week before Ted left. Many of the people assumed he was taking a break and would be joining Yvonne and the girls to make their move. As Yvonne opened the gift, her eyes widened. What a surprise! Inside was a framed picture with a clock on a countryside scene. In calligraphy lettering across the glass were etched these words:

Trust in the Lord with all your heart,
And do not lean on your own understanding.
In all your ways acknowledge Him
And He will make your paths straight.

Do not be wise in your own eyes;
Fear the Lord and turn away from evil.
It will be healing to your body,
And refreshment to your bones.
(Prov. 3:5–8)

God was reassuring her that he was indeed watching over her. Today, more than twenty-five years later, she has the picture—and the clock still keeps time.

What about the effects of adultery on Greg and Ted? The book of Proverbs is filled with verses that address this issue. For example: "But a man who commits adultery lacks judgment; whoever does so destroys himself" (Prov. 6:32).

It is obvious the mind-set comes before the act. Both Greg and Ted had already been making wrong choices and satisfying desires of the "flesh."

We know God forgives sin. As Scripture says, "If we confess our sins, He is faithful and just to forgive us our sins and to cleanse us from all unrighteousness" (1 John 1:9 NKJV). Acknowledgment of sin before God brings immediate forgiveness and restoration of our relationship with him, but we must still deal with consequences.

I don't know what took place between Greg and his Lord, but he was not willing to acknowledge to me that he had done anything wrong or that his relationship with Vicki was wrong. He never asked my forgiveness. The church board did not receive an acknowledgement of wrongdoing and felt they could not attempt any restoration. As a result, Greg lost his ministry and his family.

With pain, Yvonne watched Ted destroy himself. He once told her, "I thought I could get by with this. Doesn't God promise to forgive? What I didn't realize was how hard repentance would be after I offered him my clenched fist."

God hadn't moved away, but Ted had. The distance between them seemed insurmountable. Would Ted have any inclination to move back toward God?

Over the years, there have been glimpses of closing the gap, but no restoration. Will it ever happen? Perhaps, someday. How many years will be lost? What are the life-long consequences for Yvonne, her daughters, and Ted? Even with restoration—which may never be complete on this earth—what about the ministry to which God called them both? It, too, has been destroyed.

The destruction caused by adultery affects everyone in the family. When it involves a leader in the church, the ramifications go far beyond.

As Yvonne and I talked about the affairs, I questioned her. "You know, at first I was in denial. But after I knew what was going on, I still wanted to hide it. Was that hard for you, too?"

"Of course," Yvonne said. "I decided I wasn't going to lie for Ted, but sometimes I was quiet when I should have spoken up. I really struggled with sorting out what was gossip and bad-mouthing and what was truth."

"Sorting out is a good way to put it." I hesitated. "We've talked about *speaking the truth in love,* but I often didn't know the truth. And I really didn't feel loving! The betrayal was too intense."

Yvonne slumped in her seat. "The problem with telling lies is that it becomes a vicious circle. When you cover the truth to protect yourself, you have to remember what you said. It always comes back to trip you up."

"Well, Greg and Ted certainly became experts at lying. They lied to us to cover their behaviors. Then they lied to deceive and cover the lies." I searched Yvonne's face to sense her reaction. "You know, living a pretense was also a lie."

Yvonne grimaced. "I've thought about that often. What part did I play in holding back truth?"

"Let's go for a walk." I stood up and stretched. "I'm drained." We started to relax as we strolled along a winding river with shade trees along the path.

"The river reminds me of more questions," Yvonne reflected. "You don't really know where the water comes from or where it goes. It's a lot like trying to figure out Ted. He was definitely burned out. But which came first, the burnout or the sexual failure?"

"What do you mean?"

"Well, I have a theory. I don't think the physical and emotional exhaustion was because of the burden of his ministry load. I think his behavior wasn't congruent with what he knew to be the truth. His theology did not fit his morality." We slowed our pace and watched a piece of driftwood floating by. "I'm thinking that Ted could not live with himself. Maybe that resulted in burnout!" I heard the sarcasm in Yvonne's voice as she continued. "So the answer to his dilemma was a new life and a new woman. And he changed his theology to fit his morality!"

The affairs were not the worst betrayal each of us suffered in our marriages. There were more secrets, more lies, and more painful things—significantly more difficult to bear than infidelity.

CHAPTER 5

Our Children— How Could You?

Worse than betrayal

Joanne:

There were some red flags, but I didn't see them. I had no reason to suspect this, and it wouldn't have fit into the world I lived in. Sadly, I was protecting our image of a wonderful family when I really needed to be protecting my daughters. Protect them from their father? He *is* their protector! I didn't know he was also their abuser.

Thinking back, there were some incidents that might have clued me in had I suspected what I now know. For instance, there was the weekend we spent at a cabin. I was asleep only a short time when a terrifying scream split the silence. I sat straight up in bed and gasped, "What was that?"

Greg was already out of bed and into the hall, flipping on lights as he went. I hurried after him, my heart pounding so hard that I could hardly breathe. We were spending the weekend at a getaway cabin in the north woods, and we had stayed up late playing games and eating popcorn. Our cabin was the only occupied one on a small lake. When we turned off the lights and went to bed, the stillness and pitch-black darkness were almost smothering.

I heard a second bone-chilling cry of pure terror and then silence. By this time we had located the source. It came from Alexi's and Kari's room; they were sharing a double bed. We raced into the room, not knowing what to expect. I was amazed to see that Alexi was sleeping soundly, but Kari was sitting up in bed, staring with sleepwalker eyes at something only she could see.

"What's wrong, Kari?" I said softly, not wanting to add to her fright. "Are you okay?" I was sure she had been having a nightmare. She muttered something I couldn't understand while lying back down and was soon breathing slowly and deeply, hopefully sinking into untroubled sleep.

The adrenaline racing through our bodies made it difficult for Greg and me to go back to sleep. I lay in bed thinking about the terror in Kari's voice. We were used to Kari's nighttime anxieties, manifested by her occasional sleepwalking and, more often, her wild talking and frenzied gestures as if she were pushing something away from her. She never remembered anything the next day. She probably wouldn't remember this either. Why was she doing this? Was something disturbing her so much that the tension was showing itself at night in dreams? I told myself it was probably just the way she dealt with normal childhood fears.

Then there were Alexi's problems. She was becoming increasingly fearful of going to bed at night. When she was two and three years old, she often came into our room in the middle of the night. "I'm afraid. Can I sleep with you?"

I knew this was somewhat common in children that age, and I was very willing to let her sleep beside me. Sometimes I carried her back to her own bed after she fell asleep.

Greg disagreed with my decision. "You're just spoiling her. She needs to learn to sleep in her own bed."

If he woke up when she came into the room, he told her sternly to go back to bed. She did, but sometimes I could hear her quiet sobs. Fear of Greg's temper kept me from objecting and made me feel helpless.

I hoped she would be okay as she got older, but instead, her night fears began to spill over into other areas of her life. She continued to have trouble at night, even sleeping with a light on and the dog in her room. She loved school and playing the piano, but was so afraid of giving a report or playing in a recital that she would throw up and run a fever. She spent quantities of time alone, reading in her bedroom.

When Greg and I separated the first time, I became even more concerned about Alexi. This was my choice and hard to explain to an eight-year-old. I couldn't have gotten through that time without the help of my own father. My mother had died the year before, so my father, a retired pastor, came to stay with us after Greg moved out. The girls loved their grandpa, and his cheerful presence in our home helped take some of the trauma away. He added stability and no stress—exactly what they needed. His absolute trust in the Lord for every situation calmed my turbulent thoughts.

I was full of doubts; Dad was full of faith. I saw this as a terrible end to dreams; Dad saw it as opportunity to learn greater trust. I was angry at God; Dad awoke every morning, praising the goodness of God. Dad was very aware of my suffering, and his compassion was spoken, felt, and readily available. But he refused to look at this as defeat.

Alexi came running into the house one day from the backyard while he was staying with us. "Grandpa, I need you. There's a baby robin in the yard and it's just sitting in the grass. I don't think it can fly. What should we do?"

He went out to the yard with her, and the next thing I knew, there was a box in the garage with a baby robin huddled down in a human-made nest of twigs and grasses. Every day for the next couple of weeks Alexi and her grandpa would dig up worms from the little garden area in our yard and feed the robin. It was a wonderful project that Alexi could focus on during those difficult days.

They were difficult days, but the tension and stress-filled atmosphere Greg so often brought into our home was not there. We all felt as though we could breathe again. In recent years, Emily told me how fearful, even terrorized, she felt by her father's irrational outbursts. She reminded me of the time the girls were playing outside a cabin we had rented one weekend. The dog's leash disappeared, and Greg demanded that the girls find it. Emily shivered, "I can still hear him yelling at us: 'You *will* find that leash! I don't care if it is getting dark; no one gets supper until the leash is found.'"

"Mom, I was so scared, I wanted to run away and hide somewhere. I thought we would never find the leash and Dad would make us stay out all night. Even when he finally let us come in for supper, I didn't want to eat. I wanted to cry because I was still scared. But I was afraid to."

I vividly recalled that night at the supper table. There were four silent little girls, and Greg. He didn't even notice how miserable they were. There were many similar abusive incidents, and they all contributed to my final separation and divorce. However, the painful scars do not just fade away. The girls continue to struggle with the after-effects of their devastating childhood.

Shortly after Greg and I divorced, Kari began to experience flash-backs. Married with two children, Kari and her husband, Dean, lived three hundred miles away. They were struggling in their marriage and had decided to seek help from a counselor. It was in the counselor's office that Kari started exhibiting deep-seated fear when examining her childhood. She seemed to bump up against something so terrifying that her mind shut down. She compared it to opening a door just a crack, then backing away from something beyond the door that was too frightening to see.

The counselor decided to set the marriage counseling aside temporarily and work with Kari on whatever was *beyond the door*. Nothing became clear, and with no breakthrough, Kari went into clinical depression. She agreed to enter a mental health clinic for two weeks to see if a concentrated effort by psychologists and doctors could help her.

The clinic was in another state, but I called her regularly to offer support and comfort. She had to use a public phone in the hallway near her room. One Sunday afternoon, as our conversation went on, I felt increasingly uneasy. She answered my questions in one-word answers and was strangely quiet. Her behavior puzzled me; it was not like her at all. I asked, "Kari, are you okay? Is anything wrong?"

After a long moment of silence, she screamed—the same shattering scream I had heard that night in the cabin. I heard a loud thud as she dropped the receiver, and her screams receded as she fled down the hallway.

I waited anxiously for someone to tell me what had happened. Finally an attendant picked up the receiver and reassured me that Kari was okay. She was lying down in her room, surrounded by staff people. I realized then that somehow there was a connection between what her conscious mind was trying to remember and not remember all at the same time and her disturbing night-time activities as a child.

In later conversations she told me that she had been feeling heavy and depressed all day and a feeling of horror had suddenly overwhelmed her. "Mom, I could hear myself screaming, but I didn't feel in control of what was happening."

At the end of her stay in the clinic, the doctors were sure she had been sexually molested as a young child. She exhibited all the behaviors and reactions of someone who has been abused.

When I heard this I thought, *Who would violate an innocent child in this way?* Then, *Who would violate* my *child without my knowing about it?* I started thinking about everyone we knew, every home Kari had ever stayed in overnight. *What man dared to molest my daughter when I wasn't there to protect her?* The thought was so sickening that I felt no emotion. That was my pattern of dealing with trauma. I felt myself shutting down again. *I should be screaming with rage, shouldn't I? Where were you, God, when this was happening? Why didn't you protect my helpless child?*

As Kari continued to see a counselor, her flashbacks contained more details. I will never forget the day she told me about the first one. She and her husband were watching TV in their bedroom one night. Dean said he was hungry and went to the kitchen to get a snack. Kari asked him to bring her a bowl of cereal. He did, and as he handed it to her she shrank back and shouted, "No!" Startled and bewildered, Dean asked her what was wrong. She said nothing and just stared at him with eyes that seemed to be looking past him at something else.

She told me later that when Dean handed her the bowl she suddenly saw herself as a little girl sitting at our kitchen table. She was eating a bowl of cereal, and Greg was standing by the table telling her to hurry up and finish. She said no one else was home, and when she finished the cereal he took her into our bedroom—and then she could go no further. She just shut down and repeated in an emotionless voice, "It was so awful."

There were more counseling sessions and more flashbacks as Kari tried to deal with the fact that her own father had molested her. Some incidents were clear in detail and others were not. Again she said that it was like coming up to a door and having it shut in her face. She was glad for the door, because what was behind it was too frightening to face. She did tell me about one other time when Greg had taken her, Sarah, and Emily to church on a Saturday morning. He sometimes let them go with him so they could play in the church while he studied in his office. She said that while Sarah and Emily were playing in the lower level, he took her up into the balcony and—though she wasn't able to say the words—she added, "He did it to me."

I didn't want to hear any of this. I didn't want to believe any of this. I spent nights crying and days trying to cope with knowledge of something I didn't want to know. I felt as though I was looking at a puzzle in which none of the pieces fit. It wouldn't make a picture; the pieces just lay there in front of me, an assortment of jagged fragments that could never come together.

How can you preach to eight hundred people on Sunday morning knowing what you did on Saturday morning? How can you look your child in the face when you have violated her personhood and stripped away her innocence?

Every memory of our family life was now tainted in such a way that I couldn't bear to think of any part of it without wondering if Greg had taken advantage of some moment alone to abuse one of the girls. What about Sarah? What about Emily? Were Alexi's fears and self-inflicted isolation indications of some incident hidden away in her subconscious, too frightening to recall?

There was only one instance Alexi was partly able to remember. She and Kari had been playing hide-and-seek on the second floor of our house when she was four or five. She had hidden in the closet of their shared bedroom. The closet had a double set of fold-out doors, and she could look through the crack in the middle. She saw Kari in the room and remembered Kari on the bed with Greg bending over her. She could not remember any more details but did recall the terrible feeling that something was very wrong. She believes she was also abused but can't remember any details. In her adult years, a medical doctor confirmed the presence of scar tissue that to him signified some type of childhood sexual abuse.

I know that many believe flashbacks are not always reliable, and children can be confused about how they perceive things. That may be true, but I did not doubt what I heard from Kari and Alexi, except in moments of having to accept something my mind kept fighting against.

Behavior patterns in Kari's later teen years and married life fit the descriptions of someone abused as a child. Every relationship she had was affected by her damaged past. I sat in on a session Kari had with a psychiatrist, and as he led her back into childhood just by questions, I saw her visibly become like a child. She described our bedroom, the color of the quilt on our bed, and talked in a child's voice about going up into the sky while he (her daddy) "did it" to her.

I didn't sleep that night. Lying in the dark, my racing thoughts turned to God. *Where was he when this was going on? Why hadn't her guardian angels protected her from such a horror?* I always tried to have a biblical answer or verse for anyone who came to me for help. But I had no answers for my own doubts and anger that Kari and Alexi were not spared this terrible wounding of body, heart, and mind. Nothing in my past had even come close to preparing me for this. I wanted God to make himself visible to me so I could confront him face to face. I wanted to scream at him, "If you love the little children, why don't you protect them? They are so helpless."

Yvonne:

My birthday was in three days.

"Can't you at least stay through my birthday?" I pleaded.

Ted spoke matter-of-factly. "I'm sorry; my plane reservations are made. Anyway, I don't understand why it makes any difference if I'm here for your birthday or not. I'm not coming back. What would staying three more days prove?"

As my thoughts whirled, I realized my request made no sense. I was trying to hang onto a memory. I didn't want to face my birthday without the man I thought I loved. I was having a hard time letting go, yet I knew he had given me no choice.

It was ironic that our daughters and I drove Ted to the airport. We all went into the terminal as if we were seeing him off for a short trip. It was surreal. As we waited for departure, Ted held a velvet box out to me. "Happy Birthday, Yvonne; you know I'll always remember you. You have been a good wife and mother."

This is supposed to make me feel better? I silently screamed. *I'm dying inside.* On the outside I remained collected. I took the box and opened it. It was obvious that he took some time and money to pick this gift. It was a strand of simulated pearls. *It's beautiful. He wants to put it around my neck.* I shuddered, and my hand quickly covered my mouth to hold my quivering jaw. Then, tears streaming down my face, I spoke. "Thank you—no, don't put it on. I can't wear it right now."

Years later, I gave this necklace to a friend who knew nothing of my story. I had often taken it out and looked at it, but I had never placed it around my neck.

Ted hugged me and the girls. Tears welled in his eyes. *He looks like a wounded puppy*, I thought, *and I feel like kicking him.*

We all cried.

Then he boarded the plane. The girls and I walked out of the terminal hand in hand. No one said anything; we were all lost in our own thoughts.

When we arrived home, the three of us sat at the kitchen table sipping hot chocolate.

"I know this is terribly difficult," I finally said. "This decision on your father's part has nothing to do with you. You are not responsible! Don't ever think you are." We sat in silence for a while. The dam behind my eyes felt ready to burst, and I could see the girls were struggling as well.

I held back the tears and continued. "You know what? This doesn't even have anything to do with me! I've had to sort that out in my mind over and over. Dad really has been messed up the past few months. He's put himself into situations that are wrong and made decisions that will have lasting effects on all of us."

I wanted so badly to protect my girls. I thought of them as mine now. Ted didn't deserve them. I wished they didn't have to know the painful truth to which I was about to expose them.

"You're old enough to understand what intimate relationships between adults are. Your dad has been involved with three women over the last few months. I feel torn telling you this, but it may help you understand that this is his problem, his sin, and his decision." There was silence now, but no shock on their faces. "All we can do now is pray for him and hope God works in his heart. Even if that happens, the marriage is over. There's nothing to fix here."

Beth stood to her feet. She appeared agitated. "Delores, Sally, and Patty—right? Do you mean he actually had sex with all of them?"

My eyes darted back and forth from Beth to Anne as I took in the scene. The looks on their faces said they knew more about this than I thought they knew. I was stunned at their perception. "How did you know?" I blurted out in horror.

Anne walked over to me and put her arms around me, "Mom, things have been really weird around here. We're not stupid. We could tell something was wrong."

As the three of us hugged and cried together, I saw the girls look at each other. They seemed to want to say something more but were hesitant. Butterflies fluttered in my stomach.

"Mom," Beth said, "there's more you need to know. Dad did some really weird things to us. He always told us we couldn't tell or you would leave all of us."

"Well, I guess that doesn't matter now," Anne added.

My world came crashing down as they told me what little they knew. The girls had shared a bed for years. They didn't remember a lot of what happened, but they tried to fill me in on what they remembered.

Beth shivered. "It was really strange. Dad would crawl into our bed in the middle of the night. He touched me—you know—in my privates. It was really creepy."

I wanted to throw up. I saw Anne's face blanch.

"You too?" I asked.

"I don't remember much either, Mom. But, one day we were all at a restaurant, and I asked Beth to go to the bathroom with me."

Beth interjected, "Anne was confused. When we were alone in the restroom she asked me: 'Could Dad really have been in our bed? Could he have been trying to do things to us?'"

"I wondered if I had dreamed all this. I hoped Beth could help me figure it out," Anne clarified.

We continued to talk. The girls agreed that it couldn't be a dream. It had to be real. They must have been around ten or eleven and, common to childhood trauma, their minds had blocked a lot of the details.

Beth explained that for protection she finally began wrapping her blanket around herself like a mummy when she went to bed. It served as a subtle message to her dad to leave her alone. At some point it worked, and she believes her dad quit bothering her.

However, after Beth realized her sister had also been violated, she confronted her dad. She immediately became her sister's protector. "Dad, if I ever catch you doing anything to Anne again, I'll tell Mom."

From Beth's perspective, he seemed remorseful; he even cried. But it didn't seem genuine to her when he told her that I would leave them if she told.

Beth continued defiantly, "I'll take that chance! Don't ever, ever touch her again!"

Emotions of anger, pain, disgust, and disbelief surged through me. *How could he?* The betrayal was deeper, so much deeper than anything I had ever imagined. Leaving me for another woman was small compared to this. *My girls! Was I stupid? Why didn't they tell me? What could I have done? How could any parent do such a thing? What kind of a warped mind did he have?*

I wanted to kill him! Burning anger welled up within me. Indignantly, I went to the stove to put the water on for more hot chocolate. I waited and paced. My thoughts flew in every direction.

Could I scream loud enough for him to hear me in the airplane heading half way across the country? Oh, God, let the plane crash! It would be such a relief. How can this be happening?

I needed to hug the girls again. I held on as if I could fix the pain and ease it away. I wanted to protect them from harm and never let an abuser near them again. "I'm so sorry!" I whispered, as if my soft voice could soothe away the pain. Then fiercely I said, "I can't possibly know the pain this caused you. There's no way I would have left you! I want to reassure you I will be here for you."

Oh, I wish I had known. I could have stopped this! My thoughts whirled. I slowly sipped the hot chocolate and let it warm my throat, but it could not warm the chill I felt deep in my soul. *Will we survive this? We have to, but I have no idea how. It's like we're in a dark tunnel and can't even see the light at the other end.*

Life seemed so dark, yet these girls were my life now, and we would go on. We would survive.

We had to.

That night our church held a roller skating party. I asked the girls if they wanted to go, and they did. I dropped them off (I couldn't socialize right then) and drove recklessly through the countryside. I know I was driving at least eighty miles an hour. I ended up at the home of my close friends, Dan and Jean. Dan was a pastor, and I talked to both of them, unloading all my pain. As they wept with me, it eased some of my burden. This couple would be a huge strength to me over the next few months.

I picked up the girls, and we returned home, all of us aware that Dad was gone. Nothing would be the same again. There would be no fixing this mess. I looked around our home. We lived in a parsonage, raising new questions, but we needed to get some rest. Exhaustion had won, the day was over, and it would all be waiting for us in the morning.

There was no sleep for me that night. I kept the radio tuned all night to a Christian station, a practice that continued over the next few months. Soothing voices throughout the night became my companion.

I recalled when we decided to transfer both girls from public school to Christian school. Ted was vehemently opposed to a sex-education program that had started in the public school. Now I wondered if Ted was really afraid the girls would learn about "inappropriate touching" and he would be found out. Could his protest have come from his own guilt rather than his concern for their education? What a nightmare this all was. Would I wake up to find it all a dream? Sadly, I knew better.

Three days later Ted called me. "Hi! I just called to wish you happy birthday."

His voice sent a chill down my spine. *What was the point of wishes when he had just left me? Who does he think he is! He has defiled his own daughters.*

I lit into him. "The girls told me you used to crawl into bed with them. How could you! I'm so angry I could scream!" I burst into tears.

He was defensive. I expected some kind of remorse, some kind of plea for forgiveness.

"Hey, I just called to wish you a happy birthday. You don't need to attack me. We'll talk about this some other time."

He didn't deny anything. The conversation went poorly, and I hung up.

Ted obviously knows the details, yet since the girls don't remember much, he never volunteered any information. Over the years he has acknowledged that his behavior was wrong and has offered an apology, though the two girls view his acknowledgement differently. Anne does communicate with her father, while Beth is reserved and keeps a distant relationship. However, it is my belief that he has no real understanding of how much damage he caused them.

Life was not easy as we moved across country and started over. In the years that followed, I watched this damage to my girls play itself out in two typical responses to childhood abuse. Anne went looking for love in all the wrong places, allowing guys to mistreat her. Beth closed herself off from relationships and took on the *tough guy* role. Both girls took the baggage of their heartache into their future marriages.

Joanne and Yvonne:

It is in the hard times of life, the crises, the tragedies, that we start finding out what we really believe about God. We find ourselves stripped of all our pat answers to life and smug explanations of who God is. I recently spoke to a young woman who had never bothered to put much thought into who God is until she lay in a hospital bed holding her newly-born, dying baby girl in her arms. It was then she cried out for answers about life and God.

I found myself returning many times to two people in the Bible who confronted God in a time of crisis and confusion—Job and Jacob. Job, whose losses and suffering can only be imagined, wasn't afraid to bring his questions to God. Jacob didn't hesitate to wrestle with God about the issues in his life.

Yvonne and I both agonized over the writing of this chapter. I relived the earlier grief of those first days of knowing what had happened. At one point, Yvonne acknowledged, "If only I could have taken their pain on myself I would have done it." It is completely incomprehensible to either of us how anyone could sexually abuse his own children.

I know that screams in the night, sleepwalking, and nightmares can be common childhood experiences. No parent should conclude these always mean a child has suffered some kind of trauma. However, it can be a red flag, as I believe it was with Kari.

People who study family incest state that a man may abuse one or two daughters, but not all of them. He may tend to gravitate toward certain personalities, possibly a daughter who is more passive and not so independent.

We have read about abusers in the home and still find it hard to accept this horror. We asked ourselves, "How could we have known? Were there warning signs? How could we have protected our girls? What could we tell others that might help prevent this from happening to them?"

"It seems strange that you wouldn't know Ted was up in the middle of the night," I said to Yvonne. "Did you ever check on him?"

"I didn't check because it was normal for him to study late at night," she admitted. "I needed eight or nine hours of sleep a night, and Ted needed about five. We finally had an agreement that he would either come to bed with me and get up later to study, or stay up late and wake up with me in the morning. At least this gave us some moments of shared intimacy."

Her face contorted and tears welled over. "He took advantage of that arrangement because he knew I would sleep soundly. After all these years, I still feel betrayed."

I pressed her further. "So what could you have picked up on? Was there anything out of the ordinary?"

"Yes," Yvonne hesitated, sighed, and went on. "One day after church I saw Anne standing in the middle of the country road that curved past our church. She had scratched her face with darts from a dart game. It was so bizarre! I asked her what was going on. Anne looked at me out of troubled eyes and said defiantly, 'I sold my soul to the devil, and I'm waiting for a car to come along and hit me.' My immediate thought was: *What in the world are you thinking? This is crazy.*"

I gave Yvonne a hug. I could see this was hard for her. "What did you say to her?"

"I wasn't sure what to say, but I knew this was serious. I had to find out. I calmed her down, hugged her, and told her I loved her. That afternoon I told Ted about it. Since Anne was close to her father, he suggested talking to her alone to see if he could discover what was upsetting her. They talked for some time, and later Ted told me that it was resolved and Anne was fine."

There was frustration in Yvonne's voice. "When I questioned him about their conversation, he just turned to me and said quietly, 'Trust me, Yvonne. Anne is okay, but she doesn't want to talk about it right now. Let's respect her wishes.' In retrospect, I should never have let this conversation end this way. Anne's dramatic actions that day were a huge cry for help."

"Remember, Yvonne," I said, "there is greater perception when looking back."

I had another question. "Was it normal for Anne to talk to her father instead of you?"

"Yes, they were close. It didn't seem odd to me. I thought I was respecting her privacy—just like Ted implied." Yvonne grimaced. "In fact, I was turning her over to the very person I should have been protecting her from! No wonder she felt betrayed."

Experts tell us that it is not unusual for a child to be angry with the non-offending parent. Yvonne shared with me that Anne was angry with her for years, actually forgiving her father over her mother. Yvonne was defensive and felt she owed her no apology. God had to work on her heart to understand.

"When I eventually apologized to Anne, it was for my self-protection, my unwillingness to move into her life when I felt disrespected, my fear of rejection, my not loving her unconditionally, and my thinking this was about me. Anne and I worked through a lot together. She is such a blessing to me!"

I could see this conversation was hard on both of us. I pursued the red flags. "How about Beth? Other than wrapping herself in a blanket, was there anything else that gave you a hint something was troubling her?"

"The wrapping up in a blanket should have been a clear one, if I had known then what I know now." Yvonne sighed. "There was one other incident. Beth had a beautiful pink sweater that she threw in the garbage. I picked it out and told her it looked good on her. I now know I should have questioned her further. I suggested that if she didn't want the sweater she should give it to someone. Instead, she wadded it into a ball and shoved it to the back of her closet."

"Do you think she would have told you her reasons for not liking the sweater if you had pursued this?"

Yvonne sighed again. "I doubt it. In fact she might not have been able to sort out the reasons anyway. She told me years later that her dad had told her she looked sexy in that sweater. That's why she wouldn't wear it."

We knew there were other red flags that counselors look for. A child might be reluctant to undress in front of others. She might fear a particular person. Extra aggression or compliance could be a sign of abuse. However, it is important to note there may be other reasons for each behavior as well. A huge red flag would be if the child manifests seductive behavior. She would not know this behavior unless exposed to it by an older person. Some of these red flags were present in our children's behavior, but we didn't recognize them at the time.

It is definitely true that girls who are exposed to sexual experimentation in their childhood have a difficult time in girl-boy relationships. They have lost their innocence and their childhood. That should be a time when they play and grow. Their aroused sexual feelings are too advanced for their development.

I'm sure we all agree that parents are responsible for protecting their children from harm. The problem? We focus on the danger to our children from people or situations outside the home and tend to dismiss that our children can suffer abuse from the very people who ought to be their protectors. Children may even believe inappropriate behaviors are normal because they trust what their parents tell them. When children are young, as my girls were at the time of abuse, that trust element is very strong.

Parents are often so focused on their own pain that they are blind to the trauma their children are experiencing. However, they need to develop their own support system so they can effectively help their children. Doing so will allow them to create an atmosphere of safety, where children feel comfortable in expressing their fears. They need to know they are being listened to and believed.

Counselors who work with abused children tell us children often block out memories as a protective device, and in adulthood those memories resurface as flashbacks. Alexi doesn't yet recall exactly what happened to her, but she does remember (from age four or five) what she saw happening to Kari.

Yvonne's daughters don't remember details clearly, but they have experienced flashbacks at times. They were repulsed by a boyfriend's touch or kiss, and later a husband's. Their negative reaction was caused by a flashback. Appropriate marriage relationships are tainted by memories from the past. At these times, the marriage partner's patience and understanding is vital.

Yvonne's daughters did block memories, but because they were older they learned to ask questions. *Should this be happening? Where was Mom? Can't she see what's going on?* However, they didn't come to her, possibly because their father, whom they trusted, said Mom would leave them if she knew. Their young, concrete minds couldn't sort out whether that was true or not, and they were not willing to risk the possibility. Yvonne believes the girls hoped that somehow she would find out.

"So, Joanne, I know the girls must have thought: *Where was Mom?* and through the years asked the same question we asked: *Where was God?* That's a more difficult question."

I nodded agreement. "It has to be terrible for a child's mind to try to comprehend what is happening. And this confusion continues into their adult lives. If they can't trust their earthly father, how can they trust God as Father?"

Yvonne smiled. "You know what I'm thankful for every day? I watch Beth and Anne as adults. They did struggle with the contrast of believing who God is with what happened to them, but today they both love and serve God."

"I'm glad for the healing that has taken place in your girls' lives. I'm glad for the same healing that I've seen in my girls."

"The betrayal of trust is so often involved when a believer turns away from God. It also affects a non-believer who decides that Christianity has nothing to offer," Yvonne commented.

"I'm curious," I probed, changing the subject. "Why didn't you report Ted to the authorities?"

"I struggle with an answer. At the time I didn't even know inappropriate touch could be criminal. I also believed that I would lose Anne to her father, that she would lie for him. It was important to keep both girls with me." With a sigh, Yvonne continued. "I was also concerned that this not just be revenge."

"I hear what you're saying, Yvonne. It didn't even occur to me to go to the authorities. I had lived too passively as a victim for too long."

Marriages and family relationships should be based on trust. Trust always includes vulnerability. We trusted our husbands, and our children trusted their parents. That trust was betrayed. Could we trust again? Could God be trusted?

Scriptures state that God is trustworthy. So we asked, "How do you prove him trustworthy?" We choose to believe the Scriptures. We trust!

The psalmist David struggled with pursuit from his enemies and abandonment. Yet he declares his faith in Psalm 27:

> The LORD is my light and my salvation; Whom shall I fear?
>
> The LORD is the strength of my life; Of whom shall I be afraid?
>
> When the wicked came against me to eat up my flesh,
>
> My enemies and foes, they stumbled and fell.
>
> Though an army should encamp against me, My heart shall not fear;

Though war should rise against me, In this I will be confident.

For in the time of trouble He shall hide me in His pavilion;

In the secret place of His tabernacle He shall hide me;

He shall set me high upon a rock.

—Psalm 27:1–3, 5 NKJV

In verse 10 he implies that even if his father and mother forsake him, the Lord will take care of him. The final declaration of faith is in verses 13 and 14:

I would have lost heart, unless I had believed

That I would see the goodness of the LORD

In the land of the living. Wait on the LORD;

Be of good courage,

And he shall strengthen your heart;

Wait, I say, on the LORD!

CHAPTER 6

Where was the Church?

Support / Accountability / Cover-up / Exposure

Joanne:

For most of my life I had been controlled by one major personality trait: I'm a people pleaser. "What will people say? What will people think?" It's a hard trait to overcome.

Growing up in a pastor's home, I learned early on to always uphold my father's reputation, and he was always careful to uphold the position of pastor. The church he pastored when I was in eighth grade had a previous pastor who had been careless in paying bills on time and who did not have a good reputation in the town. My father was intent on rebuilding trust in the community. At times this felt like too heavy a burden on my shoulders. *What if I failed? What if I hurt my father?* I couldn't bear the thought, so I was very careful. I was sure I had the words "minister's daughter" branded into my forehead, the way the kids tiptoed around me at school.

When I decided to stop living a lie about my marriage, my first thought was, *Who do I tell? The whole church will have to know! What will people think?* I had protected and defended the ministry for so many years. I wondered, *Do I really have the boldness to shatter the illusion I so carefully created?*

That summer during my first marital separation I did find out what people in the church were thinking. I received cards from many who shared their love and concern. I also had some phone calls and visits from people who did not understand. Many in the church had seen only the charismatic side of Greg. They saw him as a great Bible teacher, a caring and warm pastor, and one who actually put some excitement and passion into Christianity.

One afternoon, Jack and Gail Swanson came to the house where the girls and I were living. They were an older couple who recently had started attending the church. I went to the door in response to their knock. Neither one was smiling.

"May we come in?" Jack asked. "We would just like to visit with you."

They both seemed tense, and I had a feeling that this was not going to be a pleasant little chat.

They were barely seated on the couch before Jack blurted out, "What do you think you're doing?" His voice rose to an agitated pitch. His wife laid her hand on his arm, but I don't think he even noticed. "Pastor Greg is a wonderful man, and he was doing great things for this church. He certainly doesn't deserve this kind of treatment from his own wife!" Jack went on and on scolding and accusing me, his voice getting louder and higher and his face turning red with rage.

I sat there feeling attacked, misunderstood, and humiliated. This man, whom I barely knew, was making accusations without knowing anything about us or our marriage. I tried to speak, and he just went on railing at me. When he finally stopped, I knew I could not bear to hear any more. I stood up, ready to burst into tears. "That's enough! You don't know what you're talking about! You can show yourselves out."

My heart pounded as I turned and fled up the stairs to the safety of my bedroom, where the tears could flow in private. I began to see that it was pointless to try to make someone understand what it was like living with Greg. Sometimes I did try, and yet the incidents I cited didn't sound so bad, even to me. The problem was that I couldn't verbalize the stress and fear I lived under so much of the time.

The church governing board did accept what I told them, partly because several of them had gone to Greg individually and tried to talk with him. He had exhibited uncontrolled rage that had literally frightened them.

I continued to attend the church after we were separated. Most people made me feel comfortable, even though some were still puzzled about what had happened. I went to lunch one day with a friend who attended the weekday Bible class I had taught in the church. She didn't ask me to explain anything. She just apologized for not getting to know me better. "You always seemed to have the perfect life, the perfect marriage, the sweetest kids, and no struggles in your Christian walk, so I was intimidated and didn't feel I could relate to you."

I was horrified as I saw how well I had played a part.

"But, Joanne, as sorry as I am about what has happened, you seem so much more real. I see you struggling in painful circumstances, but I also see your continuing trust in God. That speaks volumes to me."

I appreciated her honesty that day, and we began to build a real friendship that has been a treasure to me through the years.

Another friend told me that our friendship seemed one-sided. "You listened to my problems and helped me with good advice and encouragement, but you never shared yourself with me."

She was right—how could I let anyone inside the protective wall I had built around my life?

I still struggled with feeling left out. The church board asked the congregation to give us space so we could work out our problems, and I felt isolated. I had actively participated in all kinds of ministry in the church. I had taught Sunday school and a women's weekly Bible study. Greg and I had taken newcomers out for coffee and had taught seminars together. I had always sung in the choir and was always present at every church function. Then suddenly I was not doing any of these things. I felt as though I was standing on the outside of doors that were now shut in my face. I could not shake the nightmarish feeling. Who was I now?

My roles, which had been clearly defined, changed overnight. It amazed me that the church, and even the world outside my door, could just go on with life. I felt as if I were experiencing a death. Yet, I was still breathing! I had to get up in the morning, I had to meet the girls' needs, I had to prepare meals and do laundry, but I was living in a black hole of grief. I thought if I opened up we could start living honest lives. We could even find a small church somewhere so our ministry could continue and our marriage could have a new beginning. I was still hanging on to the white-picket-fence version of life I wanted so badly.

Greg and I did get back together at the end of the summer, on the advice of his counselor. The church hired an interim pastor and began a search for Greg's replacement. The church board felt we needed to work on our marriage without the stress of ministry—at least that is what we were told.

I couldn't seem to shake my depression. We still lived in the same town as the church, our girls went to school at the academy connected to the church, and those connections kept the pain of what had happened right in my face. I even went to church on Sunday mornings for a while with the girls. Greg refused to go. We were back in the same rut—patterns of relating are hard to change.

Again, I blamed myself for this mess. I wanted so badly to make life good for all of us, yet I couldn't. Many days I sat in a chair and cried, having no energy to do even the simplest tasks. I ran a low-grade fever for over a month, and some days I stayed in bed. Finally I went to the doctor to get help, but he couldn't find anything physically wrong.

A year went by. Greg was hired by a mission organization to promote their ministry in churches in a tri-state area. He was away from home much of the time, and most of the tension left with him. I relaxed more and felt free to meet with church friends and pretend that life was normal.

Then one day Greg received a call from a church in a nearby state asking if he would be interested in applying for the position of senior pastor. They knew what had happened to us. The position was being offered only on the condition that there would be reconciliation between us and the church we had to leave. They also asked for a written recommendation from the church. Greg went before the congregation one Sunday morning, acknowledged his wrongs, and asked forgiveness. It sounded real, and the board gave us the letter of recommendation.

We met one evening with the elder board of the seeking church, and they told Greg bluntly they considered themselves unique in some ways and did not want to change how they functioned as a church body. For example, they felt strongly that Sunday evening was a time for families to be at home together, so there was no Sunday night service. Greg assured them he would fit in with their ideas. The church was small, so the elders requested he continue to work part-time, if possible. They could afford to pay him only a part-time salary. Those were the conditions under which we went to pastor this new church.

A new beginning! I was excited. The Lord in his gracious, forgiving, restoring way was providing another opportunity for us to serve him in church ministry. I also saw this as a time to grow closer in our marriage. The excitement of the new work spilled over into our home life, and it seemed as though the tragedy of the past was truly behind us. . . . But it wasn't.

Greg had visions and goals for this small group of people, and he intended to make things happen as quickly as possible. He envisioned a mega-church he would pastor some day, so he began to drive the elder board toward that goal. Unfortunately, they did not have the same vision and soon began to resent the endless programs he tried to introduce. Ironically, one of the first things he did was to start a Sunday evening service, and he demanded that the elders be there as examples of good Christian leadership.

We had been there a little over a year and a half when Greg came dashing into the house while a board meeting was being conducted. "You need to come back to church with me." His lips quivered and his face was flushed. "They're going to fire me!" With my heart pounding, I walked next door to the church with him.

"We just don't have enough money to continue paying you," the lead elder said. Greg had given up his part-time job with the mission organization a few months before and had insisted the church pay him full-time so he could devote all his time and energy to the work of the church. I suspected they had finally had enough.

The friends I had made in the church expressed their love and concern about what we would do.

What will we do? I thought. *Can our family hold up under the strain of having to look for a new place to live? Will we have to say good-bye to new friends? Will the girls have to change schools again?* I was in turmoil.

At times I was almost glad these things happened, because I thought that Greg would understand he needed help. Maybe he would listen to counselors instead of correcting them. Maybe he would even listen to me. In the past he would sometimes ask me what was wrong. But if I didn't give him the answer he wanted to hear, he became angry and told me I was also against him: "How can we be a team if you criticize and find fault with what I do?" Greg would fire at me. "If you would just submit like a Christian wife is supposed to do, we wouldn't have problems."

Submit? That was almost laughable. I had been beaten down so many times by Greg's temper and his verbal abuse that I felt like a nonperson. I hardly ever dared to object to anything he decided.

We moved to the next town and cut off all communication with our church friends. Greg referred to them as "traitors and evil people." He refused to get a job. He'd say, "I am called by God to be a pastor, and that's what I will do."

We used some savings from the equity of a previous home to rent a house and pay living expenses. Greg sat at home in a room he made into an office and worked on plans to help churches grow.

I worried about the girls. Sarah was now a freshman in college, but Emily, quiet and shy, had to transfer schools in her senior year. The new school was much larger. I asked her about this in later years.

"Mom, I just couldn't get up the nerve to walk into the huge lunch-room and find a place to sit. I didn't know anyone. So I sat by my locker with a book in my hand and ate my lunch." She spoke with a shudder. "That was a miserable time for me. You and Dad were struggling, and I was lonely and afraid at school."

Communication in our home was not good. The bad dream I was living in kept getting worse. I was afraid of the emotional damage we were doing to the girls. However, I didn't ask them how they were feeling because I didn't want to know. I just kept hoping that this was temporary and someday life would become normal for all of us.

My goal now was to keep life at home as normal as possible. I drove the girls to piano lessons and made sure they were involved in a church youth group. I ignored the fact that Alexi was spending more and more time in her room, isolating herself, buried in books. That was a relief to me, because I didn't have to explain anything or answer impossible questions. I was also glad Sarah was at college.

We were living in the aftermath of two church disasters, and both Greg and I were depressed. Some Sunday mornings we dropped the three girls off at Sunday school and then went to a nearby restaurant and drank coffee until it was time to pick them up again. I don't recall that we talked much about our lives at this point. Why talk? We would just get into another argument.

I was angry because I believed that God in his grace had given us this second opportunity to work in a church and Greg had abused it. He was angry at the church because they were so "short-sighted and refused to catch his vision." Now he considered them "the enemy."

There were several more church disasters before we divorced. Each time I thought, *Maybe this will be the church that will allow us to finally have normal ministry and home life.* But each time, it crashed.

At one point Greg was an assistant pastor for a time in a small church. Pastor Steve was a longtime friend who wanted to encourage and help Greg use his gifts. Again, Greg started pushing and taking over, until Steve almost had an emotional breakdown and asked Greg to resign.

Then Greg tried to start his own church in the same town with people who had left other churches. It didn't last either. It was in the middle of this final church episode that I found out I needed a hip joint replacement due to arthritis. When Greg filled out the paperwork at the hospital he wrote "unemployed." The church had disbanded. I had been dealt blow after blow. Wasn't it enough that I was scared and nervous about major surgery and the pain of recovery? Now I had to accept the fact that we had no income, we probably had no place to live in another few months, and we had no prospects of a future.

Eight months later I moved out for the final time.

Yvonne:

What will people think? Don't we have an image to maintain? Why do others look to us as examples, yet they don't behave in the same manner they expect us to? People expect a pastor and his family to maintain a certain standard. Is it realistic? Is it fair? Maybe not. Yet I lived my life as a pastor's wife believing this to be true. I was careful of our reputation. I believed that it was important to have our "house in order" if we were to lead others.

My children were also aware that people were looking. They often commented that it wasn't fair that they had to live by a different standard than their friends. They had limitations on where they could go, what they could wear, and how they acted. We believed we were giving them principles for behavior, not simply rules. One of those principles included being an example, not a stumbling block to others. The girls definitely did not appreciate their role as PKs (preacher's kids). After we left the ministry, the burden of being watched and sometimes harshly judged was lifted.

Living in this "glass house" is somewhat normal for a pastor's family. However, when there are dirty secrets, it becomes a much different picture. The "glass" in the house becomes smeared, and it is often the pastor's wife who is charged with keeping it clean. It feels right to keep secrets covered up, even if it isn't the best path to follow. Even though at the time of Ted's first affair I didn't know the details, I'm sure I would have helped keep our secret from the church.

This time I decided on the truth. I was going to let others see that the glass in our house was dirty. Not knowing for certain what was happening, I opted to wait a few months while I sorted out my confusion. Ted resigned from the church. His explanation was that he was suffering from burnout and needed time to restore his health. This was far from the full story, of course, but easier to explain. The girls and I would temporarily stay in the parsonage, but a few people knew he wouldn't return for us.

After we put Ted on the plane, I met with the head elder. I asked to be relieved from my teaching responsibilities at the church. He was sure they needed me, so I leveled with him. "I'm not sure you know what is happening." I told him about the infidelity. I gave no details but enough information to paint the picture. "You have my permission to enact any type of church action that you deem appropriate," I said.

The elder board decided the best course of action was to say nothing. Maybe they believed that gossip in a small community would be more damaging to the church than silence. To me it felt like more secrecy and invalidation.

After Ted left, I received word of gossip in town. Some was about me, but false. I naturally wanted to defend myself. I will never forget the advice that Pastor Dan gave me. He shared the verse from the book of James: "Humble yourselves in the sight of the Lord, and He will lift you up" (James 4:10 NKJV).

He reminded me of how Jesus taught his disciples that those who exalt themselves will be humbled and those who humble themselves will be exalted. Pastor Dan assured me that truth will win over falsehood. I could trust God with my future. I have never forgotten that advice and have had numerous occasions to share these principles with others.

I had two months to sell my possessions, pack what I could get into a 6' x 12' U-Haul, and get ready for a move. Good friends from the church, Karen and Will—with whom I had shared my situation—came to help.

"You're not moving across country all by yourself," Will said.

"I don't seem to have a choice. My husband is gone, and here I am. I guess I don't have many options, do I?"

"Yvonne, what I mean is that you're not doing this alone! We are going with you."

Will's statement was straightforward. I suddenly felt as if a weight was lifted from my shoulders.

"We'll use the time for a vacation and continue traveling after we get you to your destination. But we will not let you do this by yourself. Get it?"

I hugged them both and thanked them. These dear friends were a great help over the next few months.

Ironically, I saved all the books in Ted's library, because I knew how valuable these resources were and somehow felt they would be used again. I felt so sad that Ted didn't want any of them. He took fewer than a dozen books when he packed, none of them pertaining to anything spiritual or theological.

I believe that parting with these books was making a statement that I was not yet willing to make. Eventually I sold some of the books to a young pastor. Years later, I use the rest of them. Some hold memories, such as a set given for a birthday present or money sacrificially saved to buy particular books. It no longer pains me to use the books—even the ones that have his name in the front—but it was a slow process.

I still keep in touch with Karen—now widowed—through letters, phone calls, and occasional visits. She informs me of the ups and downs of the church we pastored. She shared two conversations that came up as she sat on a pulpit committee.

In discussion of pastoral leadership and church growth, Ted's name was given as one of the men who brought growth to this body. An elder stated that although he did not condone Ted's choices at the end of his ministry, the church was still reaping the fruit of that growth. "He had a wife who couldn't be beat," the elder said, with tears brimming in his eyes.

Karen then wrote further. "People in our church may not have treated you right, Yvonne, but I think on a scale of one to ten, most have you at ten plus!" After letting me know of others who voiced the same opinion, she added, "I wish, I wish, I wish—anyway . . ."

Their honor and respect of me was a pleasant surprise. I also wish . . .

Karen shared a second item from the meeting. She had asked that future interviews with pastors also include more direct moral and ethical questions. The committee was receptive and discussed the pastor/shepherd requirements found in Ezekiel 34. Prayer was offered in asking God for a new shepherd who would bring healing to this local body of believers. When a church deals with men in ministry who fail, it is wise to build in safeguards.

This church was still struggling. Whenever I heard about moral or ethical issues, they weighed heavily on my heart, and I would take the guilt upon myself. I felt that our legacy had not only affected many in the church who had looked to Ted as their spiritual leader, but also that in some way the pattern of secrecy had affected the selection of other leaders as well.

James warns his readers to be careful when wanting to teach, for teachers receive a greater condemnation if they choose not to follow

God. Our final example at this church cancelled out so much of the good accomplished. I was the one who felt the burden. It seemed to me that Ted didn't even think about what influence his decisions had had on the church. To be fair to him, this may not be the case.

The church should be a place for the wounded, but that is often not the case. About a year after I relocated, I sought out the advice and comfort of a pastor. I don't remember our entire conversation. But part of it is still fresh after more than twenty-five years.

I was not divorced yet, but I had seriously considered filing papers. When his fling did not work out, Ted moved to the area where I lived. Now he was pressing me to consider rebuilding our marriage, even though his lifestyle had not changed. I needed to talk to a spiritual advisor. However, I did not want to talk to my pastor, so I visited one at a nearby church.

Pastor Larson leaned back in his chair and declared emphatically, "Your body belongs to your husband. Divorce is wrong. The Bible says that God hates divorce." I braced myself for the next onslaught. "If your husband wants to come back, it is your duty to forgive and welcome him. Furthermore, you need to be meeting his sexual needs. Otherwise you are partly responsible for his running around on you."

I met his suggestion with horror. "You're kidding! I won't take that guilt trip. What about STDs? Venereal disease?"

"You honor God in this marriage, and God can protect you."

I jumped up. "That's crazy. That's just like walking out on the railroad tracks when a train is coming and lifting my hands to heaven, praying that God will stop the train. It's suicide!" Trying to stop my voice from shaking, I slowed down. "I don't believe that God will honor any such decision. I believe the only way I can show love to Ted is to hold him accountable."

I left his office in tears and never went back.

The girls and I were in a good church with a great youth group. They were involved in Bible quizzing and had spiritual and emotional support from the youth pastor. I joined the single-parent group and got to know some wonderful people. We were welcomed and cared for. At first there was little desire for ministry; I just wanted to rest. Soon, however, my sense of sitting on the shelf caused me to look for opportunities. I was allowed to teach a third-grade class but was told I could not work with the teens since being a divorcee might be a poor example to them.

I discovered that not all churches were as gracious as the one I attended. I was invited by a friend to speak at her church's ladies' retreat, until someone found out I was divorced. No further mention was made of that invitation. I had to win the hearts of God's people by my life and example. However, I could not give up on the local church; it was my family.

Joanne and Yvonne:

Our memories of the church and how congregations relate to the wounded within are mixed with joy and sorrow. There is nothing better than to be loved by the family of God when it operates biblically. We bear one another's burdens. We encourage one another. We comfort one another. We cry together and laugh together. Yet often we judge carelessly, condemn without facts, and jump to wrong conclusions.

It has been said that the church should be a hospital for the wounded, not just a haven for the saints. Could it be that the church actually shoots her wounded? Many in the church have been shot rather than healed. It is sad that some divorced people leave the organized church, never to return. Fortunately, in the last few decades many churches have begun to address this problem, and many have made great progress.

Of course it is true that God hates divorce. He hates all sin. But the quote from Malachi 2:16 is in the context of infidelity and treachery (putting away the wife of your youth). It is not a proof-text to be thrown at people.

As Yvonne and I talked about the stigma of divorce, especially within the church, she declared, "I didn't want to be divorced. I didn't believe in it."

"Neither did I! That's why I had such difficulty leaving. And why I always returned to my marriage," I replied.

Over many years, we have seldom met anyone who wanted to be divorced. When we took our vows, we meant them. It is wonderful when those who work with the divorced in the church are sensitive to this fact.

To clarify, we do not intend this book to be a dissertation on what each individual church should do or say if they find someone on the pastoral staff in a compromising situation. However, we do know that secrecy and cover-up is not the God-honoring approach. Accountability and church discipline are biblical concepts.

There is much debate about whether or not an adulterous pastor should be restored to ministry. Feelings run strong. Again, it is not our intent to answer that debate. However, it is important to know that this is a character issue, a sin against the body (the physical body and the church body). Repentance and forgiveness are part of restoration, of course. But we fool ourselves if we do not recognize the spiritual leader's abuse of power that has occurred when he falls.

Both, of us would love to see our former spouses respond to God's forgiveness. In Yvonne's case, Ted knew he made wrong choices. He was not blaming others. He has acknowledged his failure and asked for forgiveness from Yvonne and the girls. Yet the three of them still wonder whether or not he fully understands the impact that sexual abuse had on the girls. They doubt it. He did choose to abandon ministry, feeling he was disqualified.

Yvonne and I talked about 2 Corinthians 7:10. It speaks of "godly sorrow" that produces repentance (change of mind) in contrast to "worldly sorrow." Yvonne's perspective is that Ted was sorry he got caught. He was sorry that things didn't work out like he had planned. He was sorry he lost the respect of his family. He was even sorry the relationships were broken. He wanted his family back, but on his terms. Was there genuine godly sorrow? At the time it didn't appear so.

In Greg's case, little has changed. He denies the accusations of others. Though not a pastor, he still calls himself a minister.

Churches dealing with pastoral infidelity are concerned with their reputation. They don't want the denomination disgraced. They don't want talk in town. So often, they pretend that nothing has happened. The pastor's wife is the one who suffers the most with this cover-up.

The conspiracy of silence enables the pastor to continue destructive behavior. The wife feels trapped. As she balances home and church responsibilities, she feels forced to maintain a facade. If she talks to anyone, she may be blamed for breaking up the home. To whom does she go? She bears the weight of sparking gossip and destroying her husband's and the church's reputation.

In the case of domestic violence and/or emotional abuse, many churches have difficulty admitting their "perfect" pastor could possibly be guilty. Sometimes women are blamed for perpetrating violence or abuse and men are not held accountable. Many churches are recognizing the need for men's ministries that address these issues.

Church governing boards should be aware that problems can arise with pastoral staff. It is also important to set policy guidelines and develop questions to ask future candidates.

People who go into ministry often want to help others and sometimes even "fix" them. Those in ministry are often viewed as having answers to life's problems. Christians believe their pastor has insight, direction, and wisdom from his studies of God's Word.

When hurting people reach out to their pastor, it is wonderful when he can use the Bible to provide comfort and help. Sometimes pastoral counseling can be dangerous if the pastor does not know where to draw boundaries. It can also be dangerous if he counsels vulnerable women and chooses to take advantage of that fact.

Both of our ex-husbands enjoyed counseling. In Ted's case, he agreed that counseling women alone was not healthy. However, when the situation was one that he wanted to handle on his own, he ignored all safeguards.

Should pastors have accountability people in their lives? We think so. Should pastors have women in their congregation who can be called alongside another woman to help? Absolutely! Should the pastor's wife be used in this capacity if she shows the desire and the wisdom to do so? There should be no burden placed upon her, but this could be a vital role. Should churches address these questions before a catastrophe? It might actually help to prevent one.

Larger churches might consider having professional Christian counselors available. Smaller churches should know who these people are if referrals are necessary. It is important that lay counselors learn to recognize their own limitations and know when to refer for professional help.

When the church functions as it should, members help one another. When the church opens her arms in love, as Christ loved, she can offer a ministry of healing the broken-hearted. Dr. Larry Crabb, a Christian psychologist, shares his view on how the church can be effective in his book *Encouragement: The Key to Caring.* He believes that churches are restoring communities.

Dr. Crabb states:

> The work of restoration is to help people who are essentially self-centered, unbelieving and fearful to become thoroughly Christ-centered, trusting and bold. . . . To think that hiring a professional handles the counseling needs in a church is a serious mistake. . . . Counseling is basically the skillful application of biblical truth to individual lives . . .[3]

Yvonne and I agreed that neither of us was willing to give up on the church. After all, it was established by God.

"There is a passage in Hebrews that gives guidance as to how the church should operate," I said to Yvonne. "Let's look at it."

I opened my Bible and read, "And let us consider one another in order to stir up love and good works, not forsaking the assembling of ourselves together, as is the manner of some, but exhorting one another, and so much more as you see the Day approaching" (Heb. 10:24–25 NKJV).

Yvonne and I were looking over correspondence we have received over the years. There were comments from friends on how the church board handled our situations, how established believers in the church reacted, how new Christians survived, and some personal reactions.

I picked up one note. "Yvonne, listen to this:

> Churches attract more than the normal amount of sexual offenders, because inside themselves they hate what they are doing and wish they could stop. They compensate for it by getting more involved in church work. They may bargain with God that they will serve him if he will help them overcome their problem.

"Oooh. That's pretty heavy, isn't it?" Yvonne said. "It's an interesting theory. I wonder how often that happens. There's no way we will ever know where Greg's and Ted's hearts were or how much they 'struggled' with their issues."

"Look at this one," I said.

> I believe the church leaders sincerely wanted Greg to come clean. All he needed to do was confess and take the necessary counseling, and he would have been reinstated to the church.

Another note remarked on the selection of the next pastor.

> Pastor S. was a good Bible teacher, to be sure, but certainly not one familiar with the concept of grace. The pendulum had swung sharply to the left! The church was taking no chances, it appeared to me.

Yvonne read another.

> I feel terrible. Disappointed and hurt. Frustrated, too. What is happening to our men? Sometimes, if I let it, fear just sweeps through me. God has appointed them [men] to be our "head," and how can we, the body, continue if the "head" is not "well" nor "whole"? More and more I realize how much we need to be people of prayer for our spiritual leaders.

Then, relating to the falling away of believers, this friend continued:

> Sometimes, as I've heard speakers say how exciting the end times are (and they are!), I think we forget that part of what is going to happen is the falling away of the believers. Somehow, I didn't realize how painful that would be. I guess it's another type of persecution—it leaves no visible wound or scar, but the emotional damage goes on and on. Relationships change—forever. And that is sad. Loved ones, trusted friends, maybe even ourselves . . . I am beginning to look askance at everyone and wondering who I can really believe—really trust. Who are they really beneath all that outward show???

I continued to read comments and felt the pain of another friend.

> My reaction to what transpired? Stunned, denial, unbelief and fierce loyalty to you both. I was totally blinded by his duplicity. I was utterly and totally behind him until the truth finally came through to me. Then I had profound hatred for him. I had a great sense of shame and embarrassment over my stupidity.

Yvonne shared that when trust is broken, it takes time to heal. Another letter stated:

> I still struggle to come to a clear understanding of how on earth all that could have been going on without my detecting a hint or seeing some red flag as to his deceptions . . . I was disenchanted and distrustful of churches, ministers, missionaries, (and) all that was associated with "churchianity." Oh, not the Lord, to be sure, but in this earthly organization which so sorely fails to represent Christ. I allowed this distrust to rob me for way too many years. What do you think? When the crowns are handed out, will he have any? Or, will he shed tears over the damage he has done?

"Here's one from a friend who is struggling with the secrecy," Yvonne stated.

> We tried (wrongly) to protect people when Ted fell. Then recently another pastor used me for his confidant. And now, while I'm not actively trying to keep this quiet, I certainly don't want to be the one to expose it. So here I am, in the cover-up business of someone else's sin, AGAIN! I hate it!

The input on the effect leadership failure has on our youth was consistent. Teens were watching. For those who knew anything about what happened, it was a source of shame and embarrassment. It was costly and painful. Sometimes it was also justification for poor behavior in their lives. When leaders fall, they take others with them.

Yvonne threw up her hands. "What about the new Christians? Many leave the church never to return. Others don't grow because of mistrust or bitterness."

We shared the above notes because they offer a glimpse into the pain the church family feels when a leader falls. We (and many of those who wrote comments) need to be careful that we don't take on guilt over others' hurts and disillusionment. Satan first wants to defeat the leader. Then he wants us to live in the shadow and carry the burden for all the people who have been wounded.

We have a choice as to whether or not we let God conform us to his image by the trials he allows in our lives. First Peter (a book that addresses suffering) ends with a promise from God to believers: ". . . may the God of all grace, who called us to his eternal glory by Christ Jesus, after you have suffered a while, perfect, establish, strengthen and settle you" (1 Pet. 5:10 NKJV).

CHAPTER 7

Am I Abandoned?

Sorting out the feelings

Joanne:

I stood alone inside the entrance to the shopping mall. It was late afternoon and getting dark. A few snowflakes drifted down outside. I
shivered. Where was Greg? He should have pulled up in the car by now. We
had been shopping together, and he had said he would get the car and pick
me up so I wouldn't have to walk across the parking lot in the cold. Most of
the stores were closing and turning off their lights. Even the mall entrance
suddenly went dark. I noticed that all the shoppers seemed to have left, and
I began to feel lost and very cold. Where was my husband? Why wasn't he
coming for me? Darkness closed in on me. I had never felt so alone, and I
knew he wasn't coming. What should I do?

I woke up knowing I had had that dream again. I had this dream often
after the divorce. There was also another dream. This time Greg and
I were at someone's house, attending a party. We entered the house
together and then were separated by a crowd of people. I kept going

from room to room, looking for Greg. Every time I asked someone if he or she had seen him, that person either said no or remarked vaguely that he or she thought Greg was in another room. I never found him before I woke up.

I had been married for twenty-five years, and one of the natural consequences of suffering separation was a feeling of abandonment. I felt it when I went to bed at night and when I woke up in the morning. I felt it when I brought the groceries home from the store and put them away myself. I felt it when I was invited to a friend's home for dinner and all the other people there were married couples. The word "alone" became my partner—it echoed in my head all the time.

When my youngest daughter, Alexi, started college, I was the one who had to drive two hundred miles to take her there and make sure everything was in order financially. I had to make sure the car had an oil change and the gas tank was full. These were all things my husband had done before. It was all new territory for me, and I was scared. Of course I got lost trying to find the college and had to stop and ask directions. I was so tense and stressed that I wanted to cry. But I didn't want Alexi to see how scared I really was—scared and angry that I had been abandoned.

That same fall, Emily got married, leaving me alone in the apartment. It was a big adjustment. I clearly remember the first night after Emily's wedding. Alexi had come for the wedding and had gone back to school the same day. I lay in the darkness in complete silence; I felt totally alone—abandoned! This was a nightmare, unreal and yet real. Where was God? Why did he let this happen to me?

Looking back at that time, I know where God was—he was right there beside me. I know that when God makes a promise he is faithful to keep it. He says, "I will never leave you nor forsake you" (Heb. 13:5 NKJV), and he never does. But my faith needed to grow, and he allowed me to stumble around in my own misery, focus on my discomfort, and feel terribly sorry for myself. I have learned that God promises to comfort but does not promise to make us comfortable. Being a Christian means being completely dependent on God, and that dependence happens when we realize he is sufficient. There is nothing else we need. But that doesn't happen in a day; it happens through the circumstances and trials of life.

I learned this a little at a time. I got up one bitterly cold morning in January to go to work and discovered that mixed sleet and rain had fallen during the night and everything was covered with a solid sheet of ice. My car was parked outside, and it took me a good hour to chip ice from the windshield and unlock the car doors. All the time I was chipping away, my thoughts were churning with resentment. *Greg should be here helping me. Why do I have to do everything by myself? Husbands and wives get to share the work of the home, but I have no one to help me.*

When I moved across the country to be with Kari and her family, I packed my things, closed up the apartment, and made the trip alone. There were major decisions to face in the next few months. I had to find a place to live, start a new job, look into insurance—medical, car, and home—and take care of all the details of starting a new life. I know that single people everywhere do these things, but I had married after college and had never had the experience of living on my own.

In looking back, however, I can see that God was never absent, and he showed his faithfulness in many ways. I will always remember the week I moved near Kari. I found an apartment not far from her. It was on the third floor, and there were no elevators in the building. The men in the church came and carried furniture up the stairs on a Friday, but I carried up many of the boxes. Saturday morning I woke up with a throbbing, swollen knee. I could barely walk. I called the rheumatology clinic where I had scheduled a future appointment. They told me that because it was a Saturday I would need to go to the hospital emergency room and their on-call doctor would meet me. As this doctor and I talked that morning about my arthritis and a little of my history, I was impressed with his kindness and skill in aspirating my knee. He suggested that since he now knew my history and had treated me that I could just continue with him as my doctor. I was quick to agree. It wasn't long before he shared his testimony of a personal belief in Jesus Christ. He has been my doctor for fifteen years now, and I am convinced God's hand was even in this choice of a doctor.

It was also about the time I moved that I began having problems with episodes of an irregular heartbeat. I usually ended up in the hospital emergency room for a procedure to shock my heart back into regular rhythm. If it happened during the day, I asked a friend to go with me. It meant that person would have to spend a few hours in the waiting room. These were times I missed a husband who could be at my side.

One night I woke up abruptly with my heart pounding and jumping. I looked at the clock—it was 2:30 A.M. *Who can I call? Who wants to climb out of a warm bed on a cold night and sit in a hospital waiting room for hours? Only a husband or wife! Where's mine?*

I dressed quickly and drove myself to the hospital. I wasn't about to use friends that way. Of course I didn't get away with that. One friend, Janie, scolded me when she found out what I had done. "From now on, you *will* call me, no matter what time it is! I don't ever want to hear that you drove yourself to the hospital."

My widowed sister and I joke about being *alone* when we occasionally go out for lunch together. We watch couples talking, laughing, and sometimes holding hands.

"Oh, they probably just had a big fight and this is make-up time," I insist, then laugh.

My sister grins and says, "Let's walk by the table and mumble, 'that's disgusting.'" We use humor to soften our own awareness that neither of us has that special person.

Yvonne:

Bill, my second husband, and I were shopping in a large mall. Since we were going to different shops and needed different things, Bill thought it would be a great idea to meet at a restaurant in an hour.

Uneasiness overwhelmed me. I suddenly felt like a little girl who didn't want Mommy out of her sight. I sensed my insecurity even though I didn't understand it.

"No! Don't ask me to do that. I'd rather come with you," I begged.

Bill looked puzzled. "That doesn't make any sense. Think of how much time we'll save by you getting your things and me getting mine. It'll make this whole day go faster."

I tried to sort out my feelings of panic. Why did this matter to me? Rationally, I knew Bill would be at the restaurant in one hour. He was right, of course, that it made sense to split up. I knew there was more to this sense of fear than the size of the mall. When I went to the mall by myself, I just went about what I needed. Even if I went with friends, we would decide on a meeting point, and I was comfortable.

Why did it matter that Bill stay by my side? I trusted him completely. We were both fully capable of making purchasing decisions. We were organized and efficient as we went about daily tasks. Neither of us showed insecurity in functioning normally throughout any given day. Clearly, I was dealing with abandonment issues related to my past.

I thought of another time when I experienced fear and abandonment. I had flown across the country to visit a friend. On the return trip I needed to transfer at a large airport with which I was not familiar. I ended up helping a teen find her way from one concourse to another. Then I boarded the wrong plane. By the time I realized this, I nearly missed my connection. When I arrived at my home airport, I was really looking forward to walking off the plane into the arms of my husband, Bill. He wasn't there. *Oh well,* I thought, *he's probably standing at the baggage claim.* I scanned the crowd and still didn't find him. Disappointed, I walked to the nearest phone. No answer at home would reassure me that he was tied up in traffic and would be there shortly. The phone rang twice, and then I heard Bill say, "Hello."

"Bill?" *I can't believe I'm hearing his voice. It would have been a relief to get the machine. How could he do this to me?* I felt confused and betrayed.

"Hi, Honey, how's it going?" Bill asked much more cheerfully than I could imagine, considering the situation.

Doesn't he get it? My voice was etched with anxiety by this time. "Do you know where I am?"

"No, where are you? Is something wrong?"

"I'm at the airport—waiting for you to pick me up," I said icily.

"Oh, I'm so sorry. I thought you were coming in tomorrow. Well," he said apologetically, "try to hang in there, OK? I'm leaving immediately. It'll take me about an hour."

I tried to speak calmly, though I was shaking.

Bill must have sensed the insecurity in my voice, as he tried to assure me. "Honey, I love you! I've missed you terribly, and I'm sorry I goofed on your pick-up day."

I knew he meant it, and it helped a little. We agreed on an exact pick-up spot so we couldn't miss each other.

I gathered my luggage, walked to the nearest restroom for some privacy, and fell apart. I sobbed uncontrollably for several minutes. Drained emotionally, I washed my face, pulled myself together, and walked to the area where we were to meet. True to his word, Bill pulled up shortly. As he got out of the car to help me with my luggage, he took me in his arms and held me. I clung desperately to him and wouldn't let him go for the longest time.

On our way home from the airport, Bill and I talked about these feelings.

"You wouldn't have believed it. I couldn't stop sobbing. Everyone in the bathroom probably thought someone had just died." I laughed.

"Yvonne, I can imagine. I saw you do that one other time. Do you remember?"

"Only one time?" I teased. "I guess that says something about me. You mean the time I was sitting on the steps at your house and I blubbered all over. I was really embarrassed, 'cause I was still trying to impress you! I felt like a fool."

"I know you did." Bill reached across the car seat and took my hand. "We'd been seeing each other for over a year, and I'd never seen you cry. I'd seen you discouraged, frustrated, depressed—even angry. I'd seen you shred a Styrofoam cup without even knowing it. But I'd never seen you cry."

"Yes, I remember. You told me, 'Cry! Cry some more! Keep crying for as long as you like.' I loved you for that. I still do, you know." I caressed his hand.

"It drains you emotionally! I've been there too, you know. Yet it's refreshing—invigorating, cleansing." Bill paused, looked at me with a twinkle in his eye and said, "Let's stop for ice cream."

"Oh, that'll make up for it. I didn't feel invigorated today. I felt abandoned!"

We both realized this was the real issue. Though it's a pretty big mistake to not pick your wife up at the airport, it's not the end of the world. Normally, we both would have handled that kind of a mishap and even been able to laugh about it, but not this day. I was suffering the trauma of a long history of feeling abandoned.

I felt abandoned when Ted said he was leaving me for another woman. He announced it. He packed. He left. He wouldn't even wait for my birthday.

I felt abandoned when I moved clear across the country by myself. If Will and Karen had not insisted on helping me with this trip, it would have been even worse.

I felt abandoned when Ted resigned the three positions he had held during his ministry years without discussing the situation with me first. I understand that each time his hand was forced, but I was offended he made the decision without talking it over with me.

I felt abandoned when he transferred his emotional attachments to other women time and time again. It created a distance that I can't explain. I sense my feelings stemmed from my perception of his not needing me in his life. I was handy to have around, like a good friend.

I realized that Beth and Anne also suffered from abandonment feelings. They felt abandoned by me when I didn't protect them from their father. Of course, I didn't know they needed protecting. But the feelings were just as real. They felt abandoned when Dad left our family. He never even mentioned visiting. He said he wasn't coming back.

They felt abandoned each time their dad missed an important event, such as high school graduation. Though he moved for a time to the state where we lived, he has since made moves to other parts of the country. Each time was for his own advantage, not to be near his daughters. As adults, they generally see him once a year.

Bill has helped me so much to overcome my abandonment issues. He understands when he sees the insecurity that crops up occasionally. He has also become a dad to the girls. They are adults with children of their own and still see him as a stable force in their lives (and in mine). Beth sent Bill a card one Father's Day and told him that he had restored her faith in men. Bill was thrilled when Anne asked if she could call him "Dad."

Where are you, God? Have you abandoned me also? I often asked these questions. Sometimes I did feel God's presence. Other times it seemed as if no one was out there. The sense of loss and loneliness was often greater than I could handle. The process of coming to grips with all of this took time. There were no instant fixes.

At one point in my journey, I saw an artist's rendition of peace that has stayed close to my heart. The whole painting was of a tumultuous waterfall. I could hear the rushing water as I gazed into the fury. At the side of the picture was a pine tree with its roots entwined into the rocky hillside. A branch extended over the raging waters, and woven carefully in the branch was a bird's nest. Baby birds were nestled in the soft down. The mother bird sat on the branch without a care and watched over her young fledglings. There was no panic from the surrounding fury.

The painting spoke to my heart. I could abandon my soul to the nest of God's care and rest as he spread his wings over me. I realize that he never promised to take me out of the storms of life but promised to go into them with me. I know that sometimes he calms the storm, and sometimes he calms his child.

❦

Joanne and Yvonne:

Yvonne and I talked about the feelings of loneliness and abandonment that we both experienced. We discussed how the experiences of our lives have such an influence on who we are and how we react to a situation, especially one that is stressful.

It is a comfort to know that when Jesus said to the disciples, "Lo, I am with you always, even unto the end of the world," he included us.

When Paul suffered because of his preaching, he encouraged his readers: "But we have this treasure in jars of clay to show that this all-surpassing power is from God and not from us. We are hard pressed on every side, but not crushed; perplexed, but not in despair; persecuted, but not abandoned; struck down, but not destroyed. We always carry around in our body the death of Jesus, so that the life of Jesus may also be revealed in our body" (2 Cor. 4:7–10).

Paul had more than his share of trials. They were extreme because of his commitment to preach the gospel. So often over the years, Yvonne and I felt sorry for ourselves because so many of our trials were "somebody else's fault." We needed to redirect our focus. Blaming others did nothing to relieve our stress. Nor did it help in the healing of our emotions. Letting the offense go and allowing God to heal our hearts is the road to wholeness. Bitterness only consumes.

"Joanne, I've realized loneliness can draw us closer to the One who fills the God-shaped vacuum each of us has inside," Yvonne said.

"That's so true," I agreed. "I've begun to understand the biblical concept that God will be my husband. I didn't want to think about that for a long time. I wanted a flesh-and-blood husband!"

Yvonne laughed at my frustration. "Flesh-and-blood husbands don't always resolve all abandonment issues." Then she wisely commented, "God has a special place in his heart for those who suffer abandonment on the human level."

I thought about God's presence. "We look at loneliness as a hardship. God doesn't! He sees it as an opportunity for us to draw closer to him. I pray that I don't move away from him after I've learned this lesson."

Yvonne asked me a question. "Don't you think the emotional feeling of being abandoned is closely tied to fear? Why does it matter if you are alone?"

"You're right about fear. We're afraid of what will happen. We're afraid of not having someone near to help us. We're afraid of the unknown."

I thought of dozens of fears I live with daily.

Yvonne quoted a verse: ". . . God has not given us a spirit of fear, but of power and of love and of a sound mind" (2 Tim. 1:7 NKJV).

"Great, Yvonne! I'm going to stick that verse on my bathroom mirror. I want to remind myself of this truth every morning. I'm thankful I have a God who can remove my fear!"

CHAPTER 8

Can Anything Else Go Wrong?

I'm not certain I can endure any more

Joanne:

It was a year after my divorce and I was teaching fifth grade at a Christian school. As I hurried up the steps to my second-floor apartment, I could hear the phone ringing. My heart was in my throat as I fumbled for the key to open the door. I ran through the living room and grabbed the receiver from the phone on the wall in the kitchen.

"Hello!"

"Hi, Mom. It's Kari."

I felt a shiver of apprehension. "What did you find out?"

At one of Kari's counseling sessions the counselor had suggested that she also see her medical doctor, just to rule out any possible physical causes for her depression. The counselor was concerned about the slight seizures or times when Kari would seem to "space out" for a few minutes. The doctor had ordered an MRI.

Kari's voice sounded detached and emotionless. "The doctor said I have a benign tumor on the front left side of my brain. It's a slow-growing kind, and they are guessing it has probably been there a long time." She paused. "They also say it's inoperable."

That phone call was the beginning of an eight-year descent into the valley of the shadow of death.

There is a movie entitled *Return to Me,* in which the waitress, Grace (played by Minnie Driver), discovers she has the donor heart of her boyfriend's dead wife. When she finds out, she sobs in frustration. "What was God thinking?" screams Grace.

That was my cry many times in the nights during those eight years. *Hasn't our family suffered enough? How can Kari deal with depression, flashbacks, two little girls and a new baby, and now a brain tumor? Oh, God, where is your mercy?*

Soon after our phone call, Kari had a seizure that lasted twenty-four hours. I quit my teaching position and moved to the town where Kari and Dean were living so I could help them. That seizure resulted in the doctors performing an invasive biopsy and taking a large chunk of the tumor out for examination. The neurosurgeon came into the hospital waiting room and told Dean and me that the tumor was now malignant. "The treatment will be chemotherapy and radiation. But I need to tell you, this tumor will eventually cause her death."

I felt myself shutting down emotionally, as I always did in traumatic situations. The room closed in around me, and the doctor's voice came from elsewhere. I glanced at Dean and looked away. I couldn't handle the stunned, horrified look on his face.

Kari was terribly sick after that surgery. She ran a high fever and was delirious much of the seven days she spent in intensive care. I sat by her bed one afternoon in tears as I watched her pick at her blanket and tell me the tumor had broken into little pieces and they were sitting on the blanket. "If I can just pick up the pieces and throw them away the tumor will be gone," she mumbled.

There were side effects from strong radiation and chemotherapy treatments. Her hair fell out and left her with a fiery-red scalp and a face that looked like a toasted marshmallow. Eighteen-month-old Megan was so frightened she wouldn't let her mother hold her. Megan cried from fear, and Kari sobbed, frustrated at her baby's rejection.

When the girls were a little older and Kari started to have seizures, they would hurry to hold her hands, pat her back, and hug her. They were experiencing a responsibility no child should feel.

As time went on, Kari began to struggle with speech. Often she couldn't get out what she wanted to say. As her right leg and right arm weakened, she lost her balance easily. She always had bruises and scrapes. She tired easily and began to sleep more and more. My heart felt ripped open with pain and grief as I watched this daughter I loved so dearly—who was so much like me—gamely fight a losing battle. I cried myself to sleep many nights. I felt helpless, unable to stop the disease that was robbing Dean of his wife; Holly, Rose, and Megan of their mother; and me of my daughter, who was also my friend. We had such good times together. We liked the same things, read the same books, and were silly together, even finishing each other's sentences.

The girls' growing anxiety manifested itself in disobedience and constant quarreling, often arguing with a mother who was too sick to cope. Dean had a job that took him out of town at times, so I filled in as much as I could. I was working at a church with the agreement that I could be out of the office if Kari needed me.

Kari spent the last six months of her life in a hospice for terminally ill cancer patients. She received wonderful care and love from the staff. I know we found this particular place through God's intervention.

I watched Kari slowly detach herself from this life. Even though she was fearful and distressed over what was happening to her, she always greeted me with smiles when I walked into her room.

Every time I left, I stopped at my car and looked up at Kari's window. There she was, waving and throwing me good-bye kisses. Tears often streamed down my face as I drove the thirty miles back to my town-house. "God, please put your arms around me and stop my tears so I don't have an accident," I often prayed. He was faithful, for I would sense a comforting Presence in the car and an overwhelming feeling of being loved.

Kari entered the hospice in May, and she died in November. She slipped into a coma on a Saturday and left us on Sunday evening. A circle of extended family stood around her bed and softly sang hymns as she was welcomed into heaven. The music we sang was for our comfort. I'm sure the music she heard was far more beautiful.

Sarah, Emily, Alexi, and I talked about whether or not Greg could attend the funeral. Alexi was adamant that he not be present and made it clear that she would not be there if he was. Dean was also uncomfortable with the idea, as he and Kari had agreed that it was best to have no communication with Greg until he was willing to acknowledge what he had done. We decided to respect the wishes of those present and not add more stress to an already grieving family. Emily called Greg and asked him not to come. Was that the right decision? I don't know, but I do know that Alexi deserved to have peace of mind at the funeral of the sister who had been her playmate and best friend all through their growing-up years.

I've heard it said that trials and sudden calamities never happen at a convenient time. I have often been reminded of that statement as I look back on all that went on in my world.

During the last six months of Kari's life, there were other trials. Alexi called me from California one night to announce that Steve had lost his job. Alexi was suffering from fibromyalgia that occurred after a car accident, and it hindered her from being able to have a full-time job.

"Mom, we have no income and no place to live. Would it be okay if we lived with you temporarily while Steve looks for a job and we find an apartment?"

These were my kids asking for help. "Of course, Alexi, you and Steve are welcome!"

They were still with me when Kari entered the hospice. Steve accepted a job with a Christian organization. What Alexi didn't know was that a few weeks after starting this new job he also started communicating via internet with another woman. In a few months Steve divorced Alexi. She was devastated. Steve moved out, and Alexi was left to cope with the shattered pieces of a marriage she thought was forever. During this time I was working every day, spending time with Kari at the hospice in the evenings, and then coming home to offer support to Alexi.

One night as we sat talking in the living room, Alexi looked at me with angry eyes and tears streaming down her face. "Mom, I will not live alone like you—I won't, no matter what."

I looked at this daughter I loved so dearly, and my heart ached at the trials she had experienced. Her faith in God was, as she put it, "on the shelf," until she figured out for herself what Christianity was really about. I feared her decisions in the near future would be influenced by all the hurt and wounds she had suffered. I prayed every night that she would experience God's love in a healing, restoring way. She did meet and marry a man a year later. He loves her, is a good husband, and provides the security she longed for. What they do communicate to me is their rejection of Christianity.

I was struggling with another serious problem at this time. My relationship with Kari's husband, Dean, had started to deteriorate the last couple of years of Kari's life.

He viewed my help as interference and resented time I spent with Kari and the girls. Looking back I can see the problem, but at the time I was puzzled by his attitude toward me. It hurt! When Kari entered the hospice Dean requested I not visit Kari when he and their daughters were there.

Lying in bed at night, grief would come crashing down upon me. I longed for the missing partner who could help share burdens and decisions. I wept for the little grand-daughters I could not comfort while their mother lay dying. I grieved for Alexi, who lay in the bedroom next to mine, weeping for her own losses.

Anxiety rose in me, making sleep impossible. The only way I could calm down was to turn on the light, turn the radio to classical music, prop up pillows, and read until my thoughts became absorbed in the story. Escaping into the pages of a book has always been therapeutic for me. I also prayed a lot in the night. I think some of my deepest praying has been done in the blackest times of my life. It is then I realize there is no comfort, no relief, and no freedom from fear except in the presence of God.

A few days after Kari's funeral, I received a letter in the mail from Dean: "Joanne, I am requesting that you have no further contact with the girls. Please don't call them or send presents or letters. I am asking that there be no contact at all."

I was too numb with grief to respond. As Christmastime approached, I thought about Dean's letter. If I obeyed Dean's request, the girls would have no gifts from me. Would they think their grandma had forgotten them?

One night while pacing the floor, I cried out to God for relief from anxiety and asked for wisdom. A verse immediately came to mind. "Be anxious for nothing, but in everything by prayer and supplication, with thanksgiving, let your requests be made known to God; and the peace of God, which surpasses all understanding, will guard your hearts and minds through Christ Jesus" (Phil. 4:6 NKJV).

Be anxious for nothing? You mean n-o-t-h-i-n-g? OK, Lord. Here, you take it on your shoulders; I'm going to bed. I did just that. I lay my head on the pillow with a sense of peace and slept soundly the rest of the night.

One early evening, a few days before Christmas, the phone rang. I tensed up when I heard the familiar voice of my son-in-law.

"Hi, Joanne, this is Dean." His words tumbled out in a hurry, as if he was afraid I would hang up. "I just want to tell you how sorry I am for the way I have acted. I am not blaming you for anything."

He kept speaking, but I hardly heard the rest. I was shocked beyond belief. *Am I hearing him right? This is truly a miracle—but then, I petitioned the God of miracles, didn't I?*

"I hope you will spend Christmas with us—the girls are counting on it," he said before hanging up. And I did!

Stress took its toll on my body. Arthritis destroyed part of the top two vertebrae in my neck, causing intense pain and stiffness. After surgery I wore a "halo" for four months that was screwed into my head in four places to prevent movement. It looked painful, but it really wasn't too bad. I was amused by the looks on children's faces when I was shopping. I could hear them whispering to their moms and pointing when they thought I wasn't watching. Alexi laughingly called me "Frankenmom," and I laughed too. It was a fitting description of the "iron cage" on my head.

A young friend, Amanda, who was just out of high school, came and lived with me, as I needed help getting dressed, getting ready for bed, and with a multitude of other tasks I couldn't accomplish alone. The screws that went into my head had to be cleaned twice a day. Amanda is a natural caregiver and the best person the Lord could have put in my life at this time. We did errands together, watched movies together, laughed together, and even cried together when I struggled with having to ask someone to do the simplest things for me over and over. Amanda was truly a gift from God. When my neck healed completely and the "halo" was removed, I thought that now life would be normal.

I was wrong.

"You will need revision surgery on the hip joint replacement as soon as possible. Part of it has loosened and is rubbing on bone. We won't know how much damage has been done until we get in there."

Dr. Nelson spoke kindly but firmly as he pointed to the x-ray pictures clipped to a bar on the wall. My heart sank. *Lord, how much more?* This would be the second major surgery in a little over a year.

I awoke from surgery with the doctor standing by my bed. "It went well, even though I had to call on two other colleagues to help me. You have a lot of screws in your hip, and we had to replace bone that was worn away. I don't want you to even think about putting your foot down for three months."

So there I was again—feeling helpless, in pain, and dependent on others. Sarah, Emily, and Alexi took turns staying with me. We borrowed a twin bed and set it up in the living room. The doctor had said no stairs! After the girls left, church friends filled in. Supper was delivered to my door for a month. Nancy came once a week to clean and do my laundry. Karen picked up groceries and ran other errands for me. But I was pretty much stuck in my townhouse, and sometimes the walls seemed to close in on me.

One night as I lay in bed I glanced over at the Bible on the table beside me. I wanted to read it, but I was in pain from arthritis and surgery and I couldn't focus on anything. I picked up a devotional book and thought, *I can at least read the daily entry.* It was a quote from the writings of Hudson Taylor, famous missionary to China. He said that when he was feeling too sick and tired to read his Bible, he just crawled into the arms of Jesus and rested. God knew exactly what I needed to hear that night! Many times since I have put myself in Jesus' arms and just rested.

Yvonne:

I have often wondered about the Scripture where God tells us his grace is sufficient for us and his strength is made perfect in our weaknesses (2 Cor. 12:9). His Word also assures me that he doesn't give me more than I can bear, but will make a way of escape (1 Cor. 10:13). I believe it, at least in theory. There are days when I doubt my own strength—but I no longer doubt God's strength. God doesn't change. As I learn more about him, my strength increases.

But how much loss can one person take? Shouldn't there be a limit? Of course it's not realistic to say that nothing bad can happen again. Sometimes, however, I feel like crying out, "Why, God, why me? How can this be happening?"

At those times he just wraps his arms around me and says, "Why not you, Yvonne? Do you think you are immune to the struggles on earth?"

As I bask in his presence I realize it is because he has brought me through previous losses that I can now respond appropriately to new ones.

In just a few years our family experienced: the long-term illness and death of three parents, crisis pregnancies, a teen hooked on drugs, marriages and divorces, cancer and other surgeries, family disharmonies and reconciliations, blended family issues, and a close brush with death for my second husband.

There was a call one day from Bill's shop. Numbness swept over me as I heard, "You need to get to the hospital; Bill has been badly hurt. A couple tons of concrete just fell off a backhoe and pinned him to the ground. He is being transported by ambulance."

No further details. I only knew that he was still alive. As I hurried to the hospital, I realized that I could be losing the man who had become so dear to me since our marriage just a little over a year before.

"Dear God, let him live!" I prayed. *What if he's paralyzed?*

When I got to the hospital, Bill was conscious but in extreme pain. They would give him nothing for the pain for a few hours until they determined the extent of his injuries. When they finished with the diagnosis, we were told his pelvic bone was broken and the muscles in the lower legs were pulverized, yet with no broken bones. The doctors could not say at this point if he would regain the use of his legs. Only time and healing would tell.

Bill, an electrician, had been standing in soft sand at a construction site when the backhoe operator lost his load of concrete. Had he been on a hard surface, the impact would have killed him. Had he not heard it coming and moved, the concrete would have hit him on the head—a fatal blow. I thanked God that he was watching over Bill and that he preserved his life. Bill left the hospital on crutches and spent the next five months in rehabilitation, slowly regaining the use of his legs. Today, only a few scars give evidence that anything ever happened.

Within the year, my mother was diagnosed with terminal bone cancer. The cancer was along the spine and inoperable. As it progressed, she had more paralysis, affecting her legs first. When she was bedridden, I and my siblings took turns going home (for me a six-hour trip), a week at a time, to help with her care. They were long months, yet I got to know my mother and watch her strength. I realized what a heritage I had received. During my divorce, Mom had become a close friend to me, and now I was losing her just a few short years later. Again, God saw me through this time in my life. What else would he allow?

Working as a church secretary allowed me to be back in ministry. However, the church went through major upheaval those few years. We lost one of our staff members to a stroke, another to cancer, and our pastor's two-year-old son (who needed full-time medical care) also died. A board member and a staff member were dismissed because of inappropriate behavior. Then the church split, which left me torn and broken. I know God wanted me at this church during this time, yet the emotional roller coaster was intense—my heart was tied up in the church. Again, God was faithful and gave me strength to go on and trust him.

Over the next few years, Bill and I dealt with two of our children going through divorce. The pain of watching our children's marriages break up was piercing. It also brought up previous pain as thoughts of our own divorces resurfaced.

Three years after my mother died, my father suffered a serious stroke. His right side was paralyzed, his vision and hearing were impaired, and he had undeterminable brain damage. Dad, who loved to talk more than anything else, could say nothing. We were told that if he made it through the first day or so he would probably survive. His prognosis on functioning independently was dismal.

Dad was soon placed in rehabilitation. He was still part of our lives and no less a whole person in our eyes. Months followed as he learned to control his bowels, to eat, to dress himself, and to walk again, though he never regained much of his speech.

Five months later, I made the trip to bring Dad home to the farm on his birthday. He wanted to live on his own, so we gave him that liberty, as my brother lived in a house next to him. He lived for five years like this, with siblings again taking turns as he needed help.

Next, I was by Bill's side as he lost his mother to a heart attack. Family harmony among his siblings was disrupted (and never to be regained) as petty issues came up in the settling of affairs. Now with our parents gone, we are the oldest generation—another adjustment.

While visiting Dad in the hospital, I needed to share with him that I had just been diagnosed with breast cancer. Since we had lived through breast cancer with my mother twenty-five years earlier, we had an idea what to expect. It seemed odd to me, but my calmness over this major crisis surprised not just my husband but me as well. It was far from the worst thing I have been through. Our family was full of cancer survivors. I was quite sure I would be one of them.

The hardest thing for me to cope with was that chemotherapy threw me into early and fast menopause, and I could have no hormone treatment because of the type of breast cancer. This caused chemical imbalance with clinical depression. I had always assumed you could "just pull yourself together." Nothing could be further from the truth. Now God was bringing me through something else that would help me relate to others. My pride was being destroyed, because this was one more thing in life that I couldn't control. My life verse from 2 Corinthians was really at work this time!

"Blessed be the God and Father of our Lord Jesus Christ, the Father of mercies and God of all comfort, who comforts us in all our tribulation, that we may be able to comfort those who are in any trouble, with the comfort with which we ourselves are comforted by God. For as the sufferings of Christ abound in us, so our consolation also abounds through Christ" (2 Cor. 1:3–5 NKJV).

When I looked this up in the Message Bible, it read: "All praise to the God and Father of our Master, Jesus the Messiah! Father of all mercy! God of all healing counsel! He comes alongside us when we go through hard times, and before you know it, he brings us alongside someone else who is going through hard times so that we can be there for that person just as God was there for us. We have plenty of hard times that come from following the Messiah, but no more so than the good times of his healing comfort—we get a full measure of that, too."

Why is all this important? It certainly is not about my marriage, ultimate divorce, and remarriage, but it is about who I am today. God, the Potter, is taking the clay, making it soft, and molding me into who he wants me to be (Isa. 64:8; Rom. 9:20–21). Hebrews 12:2 calls Jesus the "author and finisher of our faith."

Is Christ perfecting me? Yes. Am I perfect? Absolutely not! But I believe the things that have happened to me are used for my growth. I often tell my grown children that how you handle hardships and trials will make you bitter or better. And I have recently heard both of them pass this wisdom on to the next generation.

I want it to be said that my life's trials have made me better. I can honestly say that life has been good to me in spite of everything I have been through. I wake up in the morning, and by the time I get my first cup of coffee, I really am glad to be alive and facing another day.

Joanne and Yvonne:

Yvonne and I were traveling together to a conference when the beautiful sunshiny day suddenly turned into a violent rainstorm. As we slowed the car to take the road conditions into account, I realized how much this reminded me of life.

"Have you ever thought that our lives have been a series of sunshine and storm?" I said. "Just when you think life can't throw you another curve, there it is."

"It reminds me of Job and his wife," Yvonne mused. "God allows Job to be tested. Satan gloats. Job loses his property, his children, and then his health. There he is scraping his boils, and his wife decides to offer him advice."

I laughed. "There's a man who could do without a wife's input. She asks him if he still holds to his integrity. Then she tells him to curse God and die" (Job 2:9).

"Some help that was! Job tells her she speaks as a foolish woman. He asks, 'Shall we indeed accept good from God, and shall we not accept adversity?'" (v.10).

One of the lessons Job had to learn is that often there are no answers to the "why" questions. He was God's servant. Yet God allowed his testing. In fact, it was because he honored God that Satan asked permission to attack him. Satan accused God of protecting Job, of placing a hedge around him.

"So bad things can happen to good people! We're not immune." I ventured.

"We certainly aren't. Have you ever wondered whether you would have had more trials or fewer if you had handled them differently?" Yvonne asked.

"What do you mean?"

"Well, God teaches us and molds us through the rough times. But we also know he doesn't give us more than we can handle. I wonder, if I handled things poorly would he slow down the 'allowing' or would he decide I needed more 'teaching' and send me through the school of hard knocks?"

"Yvonne, there you go making it complicated. I don't have any answers for you. I do know that the times God was disciplining me because of sin in my life are not lessons I want to repeat."

"Of course not, but even when we do wrong and God corrects us, it's for our good," Yvonne declared.

The writer of Hebrews tells us "no chastening [discipline] seems to be joyful for the present, but painful; nevertheless, afterward it yields the peaceable fruit of righteousness to those who have been trained by it" (Heb. 12:11 NKJV).

Other times we experience trials in our lives through no fault of our own, but due to others' sin. Choices that Greg and Ted made had far-reaching consequences for both of us as well as for our children.

Life will always be filled with trials. Some will be a result of our own sin. Some will be the consequences of others' sins. Some will be simply because we live in a fallen world. And some will be God's way of conforming us to his image. Ultimately, our appropriate response to trials brings joy.

Peter encourages us: "Beloved, do not think it strange concerning the fiery trial which is to try you, as though some strange thing happened to you; but rejoice to the extent that you partake of Christ's sufferings, that when his glory is revealed, you may also be glad with exceeding joy" (1 Pet. 4:12–13 NKJV).

CHAPTER 9

Is there Hope for Me?

God does restore life

Joanne:

I held a steaming cup of coffee in my hands, allowing the heat to warm my chilled fingers. On this cold December morning, shortly after my divorce, I was having breakfast with my friend Mary Jo at our favorite restaurant. With no one to bother us, I looked forward to our regular Saturday morning chat.

"I am enjoying teaching again," I told Mary Jo. "These fifth graders are fun. You can give them a project and it's amazing how creative they become with it." I took a bite of scrambled eggs and toast and then continued. "When I'm teaching, I forget for a little while that my life has completely changed."

"What happens at the end of the day?" Mary Jo asked.

"Oh, when I leave school and I'm in my apartment, everything comes back. I feel the shock of what has happened all over again. I can't describe the loneliness I feel. I'm filled with a sense of unreality. My mind wants to believe this is just a bad dream. I really miss being part of a family and sharing my days with someone. Honestly, Mary Jo, I expected to be married right until the end of my life."

Mary Jo looked at me. "So, how does God figure into all this for you, Joanne? Have you experienced his faithfulness, his promise never to leave us or forsake us?" She hesitated and then went on. "Tell me if I'm probing into something too painful, but I really want to know if you have found God to be who he says he is."

I assured her that she wasn't causing me more pain. These were familiar issues that I struggled with.

"Well then, let me ask you this as well. What about his promises of providing our needs? What about restoration and healing?"

I couldn't answer those questions to my satisfaction or hers that day. But in the months and years following my divorce, I have experienced God's faithfulness and care in very practical ways. There are days when I feel incredibly sad and lonely, and very much afraid. However, it's the tough days that prompt me to go to God's Word and see what he says about his relationship with me.

"As a father has compassion on his children, so the Lord has compassion on those who fear him; for he knows how we are formed, he remembers that we are dust" (Ps. 103:13–14).

Scriptures like this one offer me comfort in knowing that God understands my humanness. He's not telling me to "buck up and get over it." He is telling me that my down days—the days I just want to crawl under the covers and stay there—serve to increase his compassion and love. He has no expectations, only acceptance.

One of the biggest struggles in the days following my divorce was the terrible feelings of abandonment and loneliness that accompanied them. For twenty-seven years Greg made most of the decisions in our marriage. Now I was alone, and all those decisions were mine. The quiet evenings were the worst. I felt shut out from life, shunted aside.

I began asking God to take away the loneliness. Instead, he gave me many assurances that I was not really alone. "The Spirit himself testifies with our spirit that we are God's children. Now if we are children, then we are heirs—heirs of God and co-heirs with Christ, if indeed we share in his sufferings in order that we may also share in his glory" (Rom. 8:16).

I started to see a bigger picture. I am God's child: I belong to him and I am part of his family. I am not abandoned, because Jesus himself has said, "I will never leave you nor forsake you" (Heb. 13:5 NKJV). The apostle John wrote, "How great is the love the Father has lavished on us, that we should be called children of God" (1 John 3:1). I am a child of God! Nothing can separate me from his love.

God also began to put people in my life who displayed his comforting presence as they reached out to me. These friends were encouraging and supportive. Again, I realized that God understands our humanness and knows we need each other. I had a new appreciation for heartfelt hugs, a cheery smile, or an invitation to lunch with a friend. I saw these as messages from my Heavenly Father that I was not alone.

My daughters were another assurance from God. They phoned me often, spent time with me, and made sure we were all together on holidays.

However, I struggled to find purpose and meaning in life. I had been a wife, a mother, a partner in ministry. Suddenly I was no longer a wife or fulfilling a mother's role, nor did I have a ministry. I could see no real purpose for living. I often felt insecure and doubted my self-worth. I even felt as though being divorced disqualified me from future ministry.

One day I was reading Ephesians 1. God says that "he chose us in him before the creation of the world to be holy and blameless in his sight" (v. 4). I finally started to understand how God sees me. I am his child, my sins are forgiven, Jesus Christ lives in me, his righteousness covers me, and I am holy and blameless in God's sight. The circumstances of my life do not change that truth. I slowly started to separate the lies Satan would have me believe from the truth of God's Word. Then I read ". . . live a life worthy of the calling you have received" (Eph. 4:1). I am whole and free! I have a calling from God. I have a purpose that exists as long as I am on this earth.

I love the story of Elijah and his showdown with the prophets of Baal. What an exhausting day he had. Then he had his life threatened! He felt so tired and afraid; he just lay down and told God to take his life. Instead, God sent an angel to restore him—body and soul—with food, water, and rest. But this was not the end of his ministry. After a time of healing and restoration, God assured him of His presence in a gentle whisper and gave him his next assignment.

Sometimes, like Elijah, we set ourselves aside, thinking we are disqualified. When God sets us aside, it is usually for the purpose of healing. Are we willing to sit and listen for the gentle whisper that says God is present and not finished with us yet? I pray that I am.

Do I still struggle with difficult circumstances? Yes, of course. The divorce was just the beginning of many trials. Grief over the losses I've incurred sometimes overwhelms me. Then I remind myself of God's words: "And the God of all grace, who called you to his eternal glory in Christ, after you have suffered a little while, will himself restore you and make you strong, firm and steadfast" (1 Pet. 5:10).

I know from experience that what God promises, he will do.

Yvonne:

God, where are you? How can this be happening? What am I going to do? The girls and I had moved halfway across the country. My new job had placed us in the city. My pace quickened as I furiously walked the trail through the wooded park. It had become my getaway as I tried to adjust to city living. This was no leisurely stroll. How I hated this uprooting, for myself and especially for my daughters.

Talking to myself, often out loud without even realizing it, I sorted out my feelings and poured out my heart to God. Emotions ran the gamut of anger, bitterness, frustration, loneliness, and disbelief. I wanted desperately to keep walking and disappear into the horizon. It would be so much easier not to face what was ahead of me. I was angry with Ted, at circumstances, and especially with God.

Having my daughters in my life was a mixed blessing. We comforted each other, yet the responsibility of raising two teenage girls alone seemed overwhelming. I had depended on the strength of their father and our parenting teamwork. Now there was just confusion. I struggled to understand how the good parenting Ted had done fit in with his willingness to walk away. Had I believed a lie? How could I have been so blind? Was I a bad parent?

I knew my daughters were the reason I must go on, to work hard to provide, to stay strong in the face of discouragement. I know now that God would have given me other reasons had the girls not been there, but that was sufficient. *God, I know the truth that you promise never to give me more than I can endure,* I challenged, *but right now I'm not sure I believe you.*

I dug into my memory for every promise I could think of that night, daring God to come through for me. Deep inside, I knew God was faithful, but I had never been tested this intensely before.

Through the next several months I discovered that emotional strength grows through trials. I studied the book of James and gleaned from its practicality. I resisted the idea that I should rejoice in trials, but I did understand that God allows trials to build character. I needed to transfer this knowledge to my heart. I discovered that, little by little, I could say thank you to God for what he was doing in my life. Gradually, I was learning not to ask for tasks equal to my strength but for strength equal to my tasks.

Reading the epistle of James also taught me to ask for wisdom. How I needed wisdom! Through the years I have continued asking for wisdom and trusting God to supply it. Even though I had knowledge, it was wisdom that developed my character.

There were nights when I fell on my knees in desperation, crying out to God. I am not a demonstrative woman; seldom do I get on my knees, and seldom do I let people see me cry. Years later, my daughter Anne told me she had opened my bedroom door after a particularly rough day and found me on my knees, crying. She quietly closed the door, not wanting to disturb me. It had a profound impact on her to see me depending on God through our ordeal.

I had to go on with life, but it took several months before I started to have joy in doing so. I wasn't sure I would ever feel happy again. I knew that the pursuit of happiness could not be my goal, yet as I yielded my emotions to God and allowed him to work, a sense of peace engulfed me.

I clung to Psalm 121, which I had memorized when I was a young girl. The psalmist lifts his eyes to the hills and asks, "From whence comes my help?" His answer: Help comes from the Lord, the one who made heaven and earth. What particularly moved my heart was the truth that God does not sleep. Even in my distress I could lay my head on my pillow and rest because he was watching over me. This truth was most comforting at night, because that's when I felt the loneliest. I would cling to God's promise of care and protection.

My sense of loss was acute, for myself and for the girls. Beth and Anne lost their father, their school, their friends and youth group, their church, and their home all at once. Most troubling was that their father had stolen their innocence. I lost my best friend, my in-laws, my church family, my ministry, and my home. Yet, God brought people into my life to help me realize I was not alone. God's Word reminded me: "I will never leave you nor forsake you" (Heb. 13:5).

Genesis records the story of Joseph, who was sold into slavery by his brothers, lied against, thrown into prison, and forgotten by friends. Later, he was elevated to the position of second-highest ruler in the land. He treated his brothers with respect and forgiveness. Yet after their father's death, they were afraid Joseph would want revenge. Joseph compassionately reached out to them, told them not to be afraid, and stated, ". . . You meant evil against me; but God meant it for good . . ." (Gen. 50:20 NKJV).

What a great God we serve. I would find myself singing. My mind would fill with songs of God's faithfulness, his healing of the broken-hearted, his life-giving strength in my weakness. God was touching me, healing my heartache and mending the broken pieces of my life.

Revenge is a natural tendency for my temperament. God was working on this character issue as well. I knew a revengeful spirit is closely tied to bitterness and lack of forgiveness. I knew the old saying that going through tough times could make me bitter or better. I made a conscious decision that I would become a better person through my trials. I thought about what Christ had done for me by going to the cross and how he forgave those who wronged him. By comparison, Ted's offense against me was not so great. I also knew that harboring bitterness would hurt me and my girls.

My identity had been tied up in my role as a pastor's wife and the ministry Ted and I had together. Not being a part of this team left me trying to find answers to the question, "Is my worth in what I do or who I am?" The struggles I faced helped me to see that Christ valued me and loved me even when I was reacting poorly, feeling unloved, and not trusting him fully. Serving in ministry had nothing to do with his love and acceptance.

Ministry had been my dream, my life, and my value. This gave me one more reason to be angry at Ted. It was his decision that destroyed my dream. Again, I needed to let the vengeance rest with God. I studied Romans 12. The last several verses deal with revenge and letting God take care of it. It also says, "If it is possible, as far as it depends on *you*, live at peace with everyone," (Rom. 12:18 NKJV, italics added). It was up to me to live in peace.

Would God use me again? I discovered that being a divorcée and getting involved in a new church brought a stigma, sometimes real but often my own preconceived perception. I noticed some of the married women seemed protective of their husbands around me. The first church I attended limited me to teaching in the lower grades; it was felt that my situation might compromise the teens. Gradually people began to trust me and more opportunities came. I also participated in the church's singles group.

I often thought of the "potter and clay" analogy that is used many times in the Scriptures. I wanted to be molded into his image. God was teaching me that he loved me and would use me when I was willing to be moldable. He would use me when I understood the Holy Spirit was the one working through me and that I was a vessel in his hands.

"God is not as concerned with your circumstances as with your response to your circumstances." I first heard this quote at a seminar. It came to my mind dozens of times during the first few years after my divorce. I know that God truly is concerned with each thing that happens to me. More importantly, I know he was watching my response to my circumstances. I know he will give me strength when I am weak. I am not yet who God wants me to be, but I am in a continual refining process. I am being conformed to his image. What more could I ask for?

Joanne and Yvonne:

"And so we lived happily ever after—right?"

I looked at Yvonne, and we both laughed. Struggles, pain, grief, and loss do not just disappear in this life. There is a higher purpose to our lives that can lift us above our circumstances.

I picked up a devotional book I often read in the mornings with my first cup of coffee.

"Yvonne, listen to this! 'God graciously divided our lives into days and years so we could let go of our yesterdays and anticipate our tomorrows. For past mistakes, He offers forgiveness and the ability to forget. For our tomorrows, He gives us the gift of expectation and excitement.'"[1]

"Wow! That's exactly what we've had to do—let go of our yesterdays and look forward to our tomorrows," Yvonne said.

"Well, that sounds great," I countered, "but what does it mean to let go of our yesterdays? I know that just when I think I've got the past all squared away, I find myself struggling with the pain and loss of those same times all over again."

"I understand, Joanne. I experience those times as well. But let's think beyond our feelings. What is the truth about life from God's perspective? I know he was faithful in the past and he remains faithful today."

As we talked, we both agreed that on those days when the past comes back to hurt and discourage, we need to give ourselves permission to acknowledge our grief and loss. Facing reality is a necessary step to healing, which allows us to anticipate our tomorrows.

Our focus needs to transfer from ourselves to Jesus Christ. We are made in his image, and it is God's purpose to conform us to that image. We can choose to let God use everything that has happened to us to develop in us the character of Jesus Christ.

Yvonne and I discussed what reflecting Jesus in our own lives looks like. What has changed in our perspective? We have gained a new, heartfelt compassion for others who are in pain and discovered we can offer comfort and understanding. Peace of mind has replaced anxiety; hope has displaced discouragement; forgiveness has overtaken revenge;

trust continues to remove doubt; and significance has replaced lack of purpose.

Our lives are tied to the past in that our memories and lessons learned make us who we are today. Our lives are tied to the future as we invest ourselves in our grown children, in our grandchildren, and in becoming more like Jesus. Our experiences will continue to impact our future, hopefully for the better. Yesterday cannot be changed or relived, but tomorrow is ahead of us. We can also bring encouragement and hope for the future to others.

CHAPTER 10

Who am I Now?

Living with purpose

Joanne:

I look out at the auditorium full of women waiting expectantly to hear what I have to say to them. I silently breathe a prayer of praise to God for giving me this opportunity to tell my story. After all, what I am about to share is really the story of many men and women down through the ages who have discovered that God is faithful. He does heal and restore. He can be trusted.

I am reminded of the disciple Peter walking on the storm-tossed lake and then beginning to sink in fear as he saw the waves. It was the hand of Jesus reaching out and lifting him up to safety that taught Peter to trust.

I take a deep breath and begin to speak. "Once upon a time there was a college boy and a college girl. He wanted to be in ministry as a pastor, and she wanted to be in ministry as a pastor's wife. It was a perfect beginning to a perfect life together . . . or so they thought."

I have told my story many times in the last ten years. The best part of telling it is that I meet women at every event who have also gone through painful, heart-breaking experiences. The one-on-one time I spend with some of these women to encourage and listen and share the truth of Scripture is a rewarding experience.

I am still on staff at the church I started working for when I moved to help Kari and her family. I exchanged being a pastor's wife, teacher, and seminar speaker for a secretarial position. It was a time of rest and also a time for me to see that ministry is not a role or position. Ministry, in all its different facets, is an act of love towards another person.

Today God has also graciously restored me to ministries that use the gifts he has given me. Promoted now to church administrator, my duties are varied. I work with the Sunday worship team and meet with the church board to help plan and move toward our goals and visions. I often reflect on the amazing truth that God moves ahead of us as we make our plans and decisions. I was not sure I would ever be active in ministry again after my divorce. Today I am doing all the things I love most, including teaching women's Bible studies.

One day a notice came across my desk that a nearby church was having a professional storyteller, John Walsh, host a one-day workshop on learning to tell "unforgettable" Bible stories. The brochure mentioned this would be very helpful for Sunday school teachers, Christian education leaders, and pastors.

I was acting as Sunday school superintendent for children's classes at the time. I decided it would be fun if a group of us went to this together. I didn't really feel I needed this training. After all, I was a writer and a teacher and had certainly told lots of stories through the years. I was wrong. Little did I suspect what God had for me this time.

It turned out that none of the teachers could go; all had previous commitments for that Saturday. I had already turned in my application and sent the fee for just the morning session, so I went alone. That morning turned out to be one of the most fun and inspiring workshops I've ever attended. I was fascinated by the way this professional storyteller told the well-known Bible story of Jonah. Before I knew it, the morning was over. As we broke for lunch, I rushed out to the registration table in the lobby and said, "Sign me up for the afternoon session. I'm hooked!" When I left that day, I knew this was something I would love to do. The following January I traveled to Michigan to take part in John's three-day training session for instructors.

That was the beginning of a very enjoyable and creative ministry. I began this new adventure by telling the story of Adam and Eve one Sunday morning at church. Afterwards, I invited everyone who was interested to attend a workshop I would be teaching on Saturday mornings for six weeks.

Since that time I've been invited to teach storytelling in other churches. I have also taught it at Bible colleges, high schools, adult vacation Bible schools, and Christian education training seminars. I have written Bible stories for a web site and always have a story ready to tell whenever I speak.

Another fulfillment in my life is my relationship with my daughters, Sarah, Emily, and Alexi. They are truly God's gifts to me. What a treasure to have the friendship of grown daughters! We love being together. We laugh and cry with each other. We share the events of our days and we encourage each other. They have supported me through many of the tough times in my life.

Kari's girls are reflections of their mother in so many ways. When we are together I feel as though Kari is with us, too. They never tire of hearing me say something like, "That laugh sounded just like your mom's!" Holly is recently married and lives near me. When she heard I was going to hire someone to clean my house she said, "Oh Grandma, don't do that. I'll come clean your house whenever you want." So she comes once a month and we clean together and then treat ourselves to lunch out. It's like having another best friend.

All of my grandchildren are my special delight. Each of them knows Grandma loves them—no matter what! They remind me to laugh more and to be silly on occasion. How blessed I am to have the opportunity to invest myself in their lives.

It is important to me that I reflect on the goodness of God in giving me children and grandchildren. Otherwise, I dwell on the struggles of living alone.

I still have to read myself to sleep at night, because depressing thoughts can fill my mind when the lights are out and darkness envelops me. I am alone in my house, and the loneliness is part of my life now. At one time I was part of a family of six. I was never alone. Our house usually spilled over with friends, and Sunday dinner was a real social event. I thrive on being with people.

Learning to be at peace and to be thankful for belonging to a God who holds my life in his hands is exactly that—a learning process.

Last year I spoke at a women's retreat on a Sunday morning. I shared with the women what I want my goals to be from this point in my life. I'm not usually goal-oriented, but these goals are reminders to me of what life is really all about:

1. I want to sit with God every morning and delight in his presence.
2. I want to be ready for every opportunity to share the gospel of Jesus Christ.
3. In all my relationships I want to show the same grace and love that God shows me.
4. I want to stop thinking like a victim and remember that "we are more than conquerors through him who loves us." The past wounds have been used by God to conform me to the image of his Son.
5. I want to smile and laugh more. I tend to take myself or my circumstances too seriously. I once heard someone say, "The things we worry about today won't even be remembered a hundred years from now." I like that perspective.
6. I want to keep the "big picture" in mind. I want to focus on the happy ending to this life—the return of Jesus Christ.
7. I want to be ready to do whatever God has in mind for me. He can use us in very unconventional ways. We need a spirit of adventure! I'm sure Esther didn't plan on being a queen. Moses didn't expect to lead his people out of Egypt. Ruth didn't know she would be included in the genealogy of the Messiah.
8. I want to have intimacy with God that comes through prayer. I want everything I think, say, and do to come out of communion with God. I want prayer to be as natural as breathing.
9. I want to know the Word of God so well that it is "sweeter than honey" and "more precious than gold." I want it to be the *one thing* I can't live without.

Yvonne:

Yvonne, get with the program. Get out and do something social, I told myself after a year of what I sometimes called "stagnating" in my apartment. My divorce was imminent. Of course I was involved at church and going places with the girls. They were teens, and it was important that I didn't tie myself to them so that they would feel responsible for me.

I checked the local papers for what was going on. *Great, here are some singles' groups, Christian ones at that. How hard can it be?* I finally got the nerve to go to one. I drove there alone—I knew no one. I wasn't even certain if I would ever go back, but I knew it was time to try something.

The first evening I went, I felt comfortable and accepted. It was a small group, but they told me of other events that were happening throughout the metro area—camping, hayrides, socials, volleyball, Bible studies. I loved volleyball, and I was interested in Bible study. As we talked together, I knew involvement with such a group would be part of my healing. I felt certain that life would go on.

Toward the end of this first meeting, a man entered the room to return a book to the leader. Little did I know that he had been standing in the back listening to my comments during the group discussion. After the meeting, he asked if he could talk to me. That's how I met Bill. This was the beginning of a friendship that turned into a dating relationship and led to marriage two years later.

Our first "date" happened accidentally. At a singles' function there was a sign-up for a group event—a rodeo. I didn't sign up because I knew it would cost money. Bill sensed the reason for my reluctance and signed me up, saying he would pay the cost. Though others signed up for the event, no one showed up for the car pool. Bill and I were the only ones there. A little embarrassed I remarked, "Won't this look a little like a 'date'?"

Bill laughed. "So?"

That broke the tension. We went to the rodeo together and had a great time. We became good friends.

Bill had also suffered the pain of an unfaithful spouse, and his marriage was dead. Though the story was much different than mine, we bonded in the sharing of our pain. We talked for hours at a local

127

restaurant, draining pot after pot of coffee. The waitresses saw us often and got to know us. Bill introduced me to several single-parent groups in the area, and I got involved, even in helping to plan events. It was a healing couple of years as I got to know others who had been through divorce.

Some time into our dating relationship, Bill and I talked about our sexual urges and our vulnerability, especially since we both had been rejected by a spouse. We made vows to each other not to get involved physically outside of marriage. To my surprise, this was harder for me than it was for Bill.

Unaware that the date had any significance to me, Bill asked me to marry him exactly three years to the day that the girls and I put Ted on the plane. I was reminded of a scripture once again: "Delight yourself in the LORD and he will give you the desires of your heart" (Ps. 37:4).

I remember often complaining to the Lord about that verse. I had tried to delight myself in him, and he took away my husband. When my marriage was falling apart, I begged God to restore it. I didn't want to be divorced. What I discovered was the verse has a lot less to do with what we want and a whole lot more to do with what God wants. Delighting in him caused my heart to be in sync with his. God can change the desire of my heart as I delight in him. The verse was still true, even when I didn't understand it.

As Bill and I talked about our wedding vows, we decided to write our own and memorize them. We wanted a commitment that would not be like our last ones. We were serious about fidelity and "'til death do us part." We still keep these vows in a notebook and remind each other of that promise. One line stands out to me, as Bill promised to help me become all the woman God intends me to be. He has kept that vow.

Bill had custody of two of his three boys, ages fifteen, eighteen, and nineteen. My girls by this time were seventeen and eighteen. Blending a family of five teenagers was a huge adjustment. We thought we could help each other, but we had no clue what that would involve. By the following year, we had only my younger daughter, Anne, and Bill's youngest son, John, at home. Beth got married in the fall after she had graduated from high school. Craig was in college, and James was off to see the world.

Life in a blended family and learning to handle each other's kids was often stressful. Bill and I went out for breakfast every Saturday morning just to talk about us. We had a standing rule that we couldn't talk about the kids and their issues at breakfast. We still attribute the success of our marriage to that weekly time, though we never *need* to go to breakfast now that we are empty nesters. We survived the teen years. Content in our empty nest, we are now coming up on our silver anniversary.

We feel blessed by God to have nine grandchildren. Being a part of our grown children's lives and their children's lives is important to us.

"If I had known how much fun being a grandparent is, I would have started there," said Bill.

We plan events together, such as our annual sleigh ride through the state forest. As we pray for our grandchildren, ranging from little ones to adults, we ask God to work in their hearts and develop character and wisdom.

Bill and I have worked together in team teaching marriage classes. We asked ourselves how we—both divorced—could have credibility. We decided we did! We have led Bible studies as well as single-parent and blended-family support groups. Wisdom gained from past experiences and knowledge of God's Word give us tools to help others. At first Bill felt insecure in any role of leadership because he knew I had more experience in this field. It was necessary for me to take a lower profile and let him move at his own pace. I can truly say we work well as a team.

Earning college degrees together proved most challenging. I had a Bible school diploma, but since my school did not offer liberal arts, I did not have a degree. I often considered going back to school, yet life interfered.

My gifts and interests have always been in the field of biblical counseling. When an off-campus program in Christian counseling opened up, I decided to pursue a B.S. in psychology. Bill, an electrician who had technical training and an A.A. degree, decided to take the same course for personal growth.

"I figure it's my best defense for being married to a counselor," He said with a laugh.

We were in our fifties!

I've served as a MOPS (Mothers of Preschoolers) mentor and worked in women's ministries. For several years I was the director of a non-profit agency working with teens and young adults in crisis pregnancies. I asked God for a ministry, and he gave me one. I was fortunate to be able train lay counselors to assist me in this vital work.

Even though I love and feel fulfilled being a homemaker, I thank God for other opportunities he provides for me to serve him. However, I have learned my identity lies in who I am in Christ, not in what I do for him.

Now we are in a new season of our lives. We are building a home—not hiring a contractor but building it ourselves. We have renovated a couple of homes and discovered we like working together.

Our goal is to continue to live with purpose in our retirement. There are possibilities for the future. We remain involved in the local church. We talk about a short-term mission trip—maybe even a year-long building project. We are open to whatever God puts in our path. We believe there is no such thing as a *retired* Christian. Slowing down does not mean quitting.

God continues to use me in ways I would never have thought about had I not been through my life's trials. A passage in 2 Corinthians 4 speaks to how I feel. Verses 1 and 16 both say, "We do not lose heart." Verse 17 (NKJV) says, "For our light affliction, which is but for a moment, is working for us a far more exceeding and eternal weight of glory." And the answer is in verse 18, as we don't look at the visible but the invisible (the eternal).

As I thought about dreams, the end of dreams, and the rebirth of dreams, I was reminded of a card I received for my 50th birthday. Anne had planned a party and enrolled me in a couple of art classes. This had been a life-long dream, though I seldom found the time to pursue my art interests. The day of the party, I walked to the mailbox. I recognized the handwriting immediately. My heart skipped a beat. *Why would I be hearing from Ted?*

I noticed the postmark. It was the same day as the day years earlier when the girls and I had put Ted on the plane. The card had roses on the front with the line:

Wishing you a birthday filled with dreams . . .

I opened the card:

> *. . . and a year in which they all come true!*

Then a hand-written note brought tears to my eyes as I read:

> *Yvonne, one of the first casualties of life is our dreams.*
> *May some of yours **still** come true.*
> *Happy Birthday, Ted*

It was nice that Ted was wishing my dreams would come true. However, I felt a stab of pain at the loss of dreams we had had together. Becoming one in marriage is God's arrangement. Whenever man "puts it asunder," the flesh tears and the soul cries!

How blessed I am that God has given me Bill. He is not perfect, but then neither am I. This is a second chance for both of us, and we appreciate each other more because of it.

Joanne and Yvonne:

As Paul faced the end of his earthly journey, he was able to say ". . . the time of my departure is at hand. I have fought the good fight, I have finished the race, I have kept the faith" (2 Tim. 4:6b–7 NKJV). Paul was not bragging. He once opposed the gospel. Now he knew he was redeemed with the precious blood of Christ. It became his life's ambition to spread this *good news* to the world. He knew he had faithfully served his master. However, this calling cost him dearly:

> . . . in stripes above measure, in prisons more frequently, in deaths often. From the Jews five times I received forty stripes minus one. Three times I was beaten with rods; once I was stoned; three times I was shipwrecked; a night and a day I have been in the deep; in journeys often, in perils of waters, in perils of robbers, in perils of my own countrymen,

in perils of the Gentiles, in perils in the city, in perils in the wilderness, in perils in the sea, in perils among false brethren; in weariness and toil, in sleeplessness often, in hunger and thirst, in fastings often, in cold and nakedness—besides the other things, what comes upon me daily. . . .

—2 Corinthians 11:23–28 NKJV

As we talked about Paul, Yvonne and I concluded that we feel very inadequate if we compare ourselves to him. We need to ask ourselves, "What does God want to do with our lives?" The goals I wrote out for myself are a beginning.

"You know, Joanne, Paul talks about striving toward a 'goal' in Philippians. The text has the words 'forgetting what's behind.' You told me that Greg used to throw those words at you, but they really are true. He just took them out of context for his benefit."

We looked at the verse and gleaned from it that we don't need to let the past weigh us down. The future is ahead of us. Every day is a new opportunity for new adventures with God. The Scripture says, ". . . one thing I do: Forgetting what is behind and straining toward what is ahead, I press on toward the goal to win the prize for which God has called me heavenward in Christ Jesus" (Phil. 3:13–14).

The world is full of dream stealers. People tell us our vision is cloudy, our goals are unattainable, the price we pay is too high. Then, too, dreams can be dashed because those we dreamed with chose a different direction. The dream disappears. Though our dreams were not always realistic, were sometimes sabotaged and were often redirected, maybe they didn't really vanish.

Have our dreams changed? Yes, I suppose in some ways they have. Yet if our purpose here is to honor and glorify God, the dream is still alive. In fact, God brings us through what he allows in our lives to magnify himself. We would not have learned the lessons so well without the pain.

We have survived. Our dreams continue. Our lives and our ministries continue. Yvonne and I continue to rejoice together as God directs our dreams and molds our lives.

"Joanne, do you remember when I told you I constantly asked God for wisdom? Do you realize the verses that come right before that passage in James?"

"Now that you mention it, I do. Let me read it to you in The Message."

> Consider it a sheer gift, friends, when tests and challenges come at you from all sides. You know that under pressure, your faith-life is forced into the open and shows its true colors. So don't try to get out of anything prematurely. Let it do its work so you become mature and well-developed, not deficient in any way.
>
> —James 1:2–3

Yvonne and I want God to work in our lives, using what we have been through and what is still ahead of us to mold us into who God wants us to be. We want to finish well! We want to hear:

"Well done, good and faithful servant . . . enter into the joy of your Lord" (Matt. 25:21 NKJV).

References

1. Kevin Lehman, *Sex Begins in the Kitchen* (Grand Rapids, Michigan: Baker Book House, Revised 2006).

2. C. S. Lewis, *The Four Loves*; chapter 6, page 169, as quoted in *The Quotable Lewis, An Encyclopedia Selection of Quotes from the Complete Published Works of C. S. Lewis*, Wayne Martindale and Jerry Root, editors (Wheaton, Illinois: Tyndale House Publishers, 1990), 403.

3. Lawrence J. Crabb, Jr. and Dan B. Allender, *Encouragement: The Key to Caring* (Grand Rapids, Michigan: Zondervan Publishing House, 1984), 132, 133.

4. Lloyd John Ogilvie, *God's Best for my Life* (Eugene, Oregon: Harvest House Publishers, 2008, January 1 entry).